THE YEAR I COULDN'T CRY

NANCY SEBERIANO

PAGE PUBLISHING
Conneaut Lake, PA

First originally published by Page Publishing 2024

ISBN 979-8-88654-857-0 (pbk)
ISBN 979-8-88654-856-3 (digital)

Printed in the United States of America

In memory of my beloved daughter, Babe Anne Rollins, murdered just before the prime of her life. If Babe had lived, she would have finished school a month later, and started her new life as a legal secretary. If her story can save anyone from the same fate, then she did not die in vain.

A special thanks to my mom, daughters, and son who helped me fill in all the blanks.

At the Start

I came home about midnight, Friday (February, 8, 2002). There were four police cars surrounding my house. My daughter, Babe, lived in the lower half of the house, and I lived in the upper half. I pulled into the driveway; the police, of course, asked who I was. I told them that I lived upstairs, gave them my name, and said that my daughter lived downstairs. The officer asked if I knew where my daughter was. I told him that I had just gotten off work and had not seen her since Monday (February, 4, 2002).

Babe worked the first shift (at a local factory) Beckett Gas and was usually in bed by the time I got off work (bartending). Babe left for work at 5:30 a.m., so she was usually gone by the time that I woke up each day. Just then, some woman came up to me from next door and said that she had my granddaughters, Taliyah and Amaya. She said that Babe's husband, Vincent, had dropped them off about 11 a.m. (February, 7, 2002) that morning and that she had not seen him since. I took the girls upstairs to my apartment and put them to bed. After making sure that the girls were okay and safe, I went back downstairs to Babe's apartment to talk to the police.

The officer asked me when was the last time that I talked to my daughter. I informed the officer that I had talked to Babe on the phone two nights before, on Tuesday (February, 6, 2002). When I came home that night, there was a message on my answering machine from Babe. "Mom, call me when you come home!" So about 1:30 a.m. (February, 6, 2002), I called her to find out what she wanted. She asked me to put her three-year-old daughter, Taliyah, on the bus in the morning and take care of the two-year-old, Amaya. I told her, "No problem. Just bring them upstairs when you go to work." She had a set of keys to my apartment so she could let herself in, sometimes in the mornings.

Normally I would leave the door unlocked for her when I went to bed, just so it was more convenient for her to get in with a child in her arms. But this night, I was already in bed when I realized that I hadn't left the door open. I was too lazy to make the extra effort. I was thinking, *She's got her own key!* So I told the officer that I went to bed.

About 5:30 a.m. (February, 6, 2002), I heard her car leave for work. When I woke up (at approximately 8:00 a.m.) to get my granddaughter ready for school, I went into the living room to find the girls not there! I listened for a minute and could hear the girls playing downstairs. I looked outside the window and saw Babe's car was gone. This meant that Babe was at work, and her husband was watching the girls, so I went back to bed. A few minutes later, I heard the horn on the school bus waiting for Taliyah. I looked out, and the bus left without her. I remember thinking that he was too lazy to get up and put his kid on the bus.

The police asked me if she went to work on Thursday, and if not when was the last day that she worked. I called the factory; I used to work there with Babe but on a different shift. I tried to talk to my old boss (the shift supervisor) because her brother was Babe's boss on the day shift. Nevertheless, she was not at work at that time, and they would not call her for me, nor would they give me her telephone number. I had no way to verify that information. I had not seen my daughter since Monday (6 p.m. on February, 4, 2002), and she could have been missing for the past four days.

The officer wanted to know the names and phone numbers of any of her friends where she might hide! I only knew one of her close friends by name, but I didn't know her last name or her phone number. Sylania was the only friend that Babe might hide in her house, but I did not know her well enough to find her. I asked the police if they had searched everywhere for my daughter? They said that they had searched the entire house. Then I asked, "Did you look in every nook and cranny in the basement? Her husband could have stuffed her body down there!" I knew that Babe would never leave and go anywhere without her children. The officer said that they had made a thorough search of the entire house; she was nowhere to be found. (Relieved to hear this, I assumed that she was at Sylania's house!)

The officer asked me what kind of car Babe had. I told him a small dark green one, but I was unsure of the make, model, or year. She had gotten it over the weekend, and I hadn't had the chance to get a good look at it yet! The police had also told me that they found a rejection notice in her mailbox that said her car loan was declined, and she was to return the car. I said that maybe it had been repossessed. I told the officer, "When you find it, look in the trunk for my daughter!" It was so unlike my daughter, to be anywhere, without her children. They were her whole life! When all the police were leaving, they said that she was over twenty-one and was allowed to be missing if she wanted to.

After the police left, I went back upstairs to check up on the girls. I made sure they were safe, warm, and asleep. I started to call everyone I could think of who would know Sylania's last name. First, I called my oldest daughter, Jane; she lived about an hour east. I informed her that Babe was missing and went over everything that I had discussed with the police. I asked her if she knew Sylania's last name or phone number. She did not, so I thanked her and said, "I'm going to call Cyndi." (My youngest daughter lives in Florida). I called Cyndi and woke her up at about 1:30 am. (February, 8, 2002) and told her that Babe was missing. I told her all that had transpired with the police and that I was hopeful that Babe was at Sylania's house. "Do you know her last name or phone number?"

"No, Mommy," said Cyndi, "I'm sorry, I wish that I could be of more help." I thanked her and said I would let her know what was going on when I found out.

Then I locked the girls up safely in my apartment and went downstairs. I had keys to Babe's apartment, just as Babe had keys to mine. I let myself into her apartment and then, *locked myself in* (to be safe); her own husband did not have keys to the apartment! I was looking for anybody's phone number that might be able to tell me where Babe was! I tried to access her computer, but I'm computer-illiterate and was unsuccessful. I looked in her bedroom. There were clothes all over the floor, around her bed, and all over her bed. In her dresser drawers, I found some IDs, one for food stamps and one for Medicaid, and I found the girls' birth certificates. I took all of the stuff that should be in a safe place. I couldn't find anything that could help me find Babe. After looking for twenty minutes, I decided to go back upstairs.

On my way out, I noticed the closet door was open a bit. The closet door was never open! I knew that the police probably opened it, but I thought that maybe there was something inside that might tell me where Babe was. When I opened the door, I saw a large black plastic garbage bag stapled to a yardstick. The ends of the yardstick were nailed to both sides of the closet wall, about four feet off the floor. I had been in the closet before; Babe kept her vacuum and all her Christmas decorations in it. It was always open on the inside, and all the stuff that she didn't want the kids to get into was kept in there. But the door was always closed, and the plastic bag was never there before. So I moved it!

There were a few large blankets and comforters stuffed up behind the garbage bag. They weren't supposed to be there, so I moved them aside, and I saw something. I couldn't figure out what it was. It was a brownish maroon, so I stepped back for a second, and then I saw it, Babe's birthmark! (Babe was born with a medium-sized brown spot on her top right thigh, about the size of a dime.) *Oh my god!* It all came into focus now. I was looking at my daughter's dead body. I was so freaking scared. I had never seen a dead body before. I could only see the back of her leg, from the hip to the knee of her right leg. But I had seen enough! I had to call the police.

I called 911 and told the dispatcher that the police were at my daughter's apartment about an hour beforehand, and I said that they told me that they had searched the entire house from the basement up. Then, "Why should I be the one to find my daughter's body?" That's the job of the police. I'm her freaking mother! I should never have to go through something like that. The dispatcher asked me how I knew she was dead. I told her that she was that deep purplish-brown. The dispatcher asked me if I touched her. *I said, "No!"* She told me that I have to check to see if she might still be alive. So, I touched her. Her skin was cold and kind of hard. I knew that she had been there for a while. I told the dispatcher that she was not alive. She told me that the same officers that I talked to earlier were coming back, and they would be there in a few minutes. She said that she would stay on the line with me until the officers got here.

I kept babbling, "Oh my God, Oh my God, Oh my God!" I couldn't believe that all this was happening! I couldn't believe that my daughter was dead! I couldn't believe *that I* was the one who found her! I couldn't believe that her body was stuffed into the closet of her own apartment like it was garbage! The dispatcher asked me to calm down; the officers would be there soon!

1:35 a.m., February, 8, 2002

Then I heard a knock at the back door. I was petrified! What if it's her husband? I'm sure in my heart that he killed my baby! What am I going to do if he's at the door? The dispatcher said, "The police are at your door let them in." I said, "How do I know that it's the police? It might be her husband!" The dispatcher said, "The police just told me that they are there." So I went to the back door and looked out the curtain. There was nobody there! I told the dispatcher, "*Oh my god*, they are at the wrong house! Her husband must be outside!" She said, "*Calm down, ma'am*. The police are at your house now!"

I told her that I had already looked outside, but there was nobody there! Vincent must be here! He's outside somewhere! The dispatcher said, "I'm talking to the police right now, and they are on your back porch." I said, "Tell them to call out to me!" Then I heard two officers call out to me, "This is the police. Please let us in." When I looked out this time, I saw them.

When I let them in, I saw the same officers that had told me that they had looked in every nook and cranny of the house, and my daughter was not there. They looked at me and said, "We're very sorry, ma'am!" I hit him and said, "You should be! You should have been the one to find her! *Not me!*" I told the officers that she was in the closet and that I had to go upstairs to make sure the girls were all right.

C H A P T E R   2

The Aftermath

1:50 a.m., February, 8, 2002

The girls were asleep upstairs. The police were with Babe downstairs, so I decided that I had better start informing the family that I had just found Babe. I called my husband, Juan, first. He worked out of town. I was crying quietly, so as not to wake the girls. He asked me what the matter was. I told him that I had just found Babe dead, and the police were downstairs. He said, "I'll be right there!" He worked about seventy-five miles away.

Next, I called my ex-husband David (Babe's father). I told David that I had just found Babe. I told him that I suspected Babe's husband Vincent, but I didn't have any evidence yet. I also asked David if he would please call our son Wayne (he was in the Air Force, in Germany). David said that he would and that he would be over in about twenty minutes. Then I called my oldest daughter, Jane (she lives about 150 miles away) and gave her the bad news. She took it very hard, but I had already woken her up to ask about Babe's friends, so I knew that she would be waiting for some news.

Then I called my youngest daughter, Cyndi, in Florida and told her all the news. She was very distraught as well; I think that Cyndi might have taken it the hardest because of the distance and not getting home to visit. Lastly, I had to call my parents in Montana. It was a little after 2 a.m. (our time), and I knew that they would be asleep, and I would get the answering machine, but I did not know how busy I would be for the next few hours. There is no good way to call your mother and tell her that one of her granddaughters was murdered, so I just blurted it out, and I left this message, "Mom, Babe is dead! I just found her body!"

Of course, I must have been still in a state of shock. Not realizing at the time, that this is nowhere near enough information to leave on someone's answering machine! *Now* I had only a minute to take a breath but not enough time to dwell on all that had just taken place.

2:30 a.m., February, 8, 2002

There was a knock at my door; it was Babe's father David and his wife. We consoled each other briefly and discussed Babe for a few minutes. Then the police came up to ask us a few questions. The detective asked me, "When was the last time you saw your daughter alive?" I told him that I had talked to her Wednesday (February, 6, 2002) morning at about 1:30 a.m. The detective questioned, "Why did I talk to her so late?" I told him that I was at Kinko's making copies, after work, and when I got home there was a message on the answering machine from Babe, "Mom, this is Babe. Please call me when you get home!" So I called her. Her husband answered the phone. He *never* let Babe answer the phone when he was there! I said, "Babe called me, and left a message on my machine for me to call her." He said, "Just a minute." Then Babe got on the phone. Very groggy sounding, she said, "Hello."

Babe never did like being woken up. If you woke her up, she usually had a *serious attitude*! But this time she just sounded very tired. I answered, "Hello, freak. You called my machine! What do you want?" She said, "Will you put Taliyah on the school bus in the morning and take care of Amaya?" I told her that I would. "Just bring them upstairs in the morning." I told the officer that whenever she asked me to do this for her, I would leave my door unlocked, so she could get in easier. But I forgot all about it until I was already in bed. By the time I remembered to unlock the door, I was ready to doze off and too lazy to get out of bed to open it. She had a key to my door, and I figured that this time she could use that!

I told the detective that something strange happened that night. After I talked to Babe on the phone, about ten minutes later, I heard footsteps coming up the stairs to my door. I knew that it wasn't my daughter, because Babe would *always* stand at the bottom of the stairs and call to me, instead of coming up. And I would usually stand at the top of the stairs, instead of going down! And it couldn't be my husband; he worked out of town, and this was not one of the nights that he came home. Then I heard a light knock at the door.

I was busy putting together a shoe rack that was made out of eighteen long wooden dowels. You have to try to hold all of them in place at the same time to put this thing together. So, when I answered the door, I had an armload of these two-foot rods (I was frustrated with this apparatus and a little pissed off that someone was coming to my door at this hour) knowing that it could only be one person, Babe's husband, Vincent. I said, "*What*!" He saw all those rods in my arms, and he said, "Oh shit!" then backed up quite a bit. "Here's your mail!" I grabbed the mail without saying a word, and slammed the door in his face, and locked it!

I have never liked that man, and he knew that he was not welcome in my house. He had *never* brought my mail, said hello to me, or acknowledged me before. So why would he go out of his way to bring the mail up to his bitchy mother-in-law at 1:45 a.m., knowing that he would not be welcomed? This is probably why I, subconsciously, did not unlock the door that night.

3 a.m., February, 8, 2002

The detective asked me, "When was the last time you physically *saw* your daughter alive?" I said "Monday night (February, 4, 2002) about 6 p.m." The detective said, "You haven't seen your daughter in three and a half days?" I told him that she had a very early shift, and that I was a night owl. I would see her all weekend but frequently not see her all week.

Just then my husband, Juan, got home. The detective asked my ex-husband and his wife a few questions, while I tried to fill Juan in on all the details that he had missed. Then the detective asked Juan some questions. The girls slept on the couch the whole time this was happening. I didn't know how they could sleep through all this commotion just a few feet away!

The detective went downstairs for a while. We all talked amongst ourselves about nothing in particular (chitchat). Then he came back upstairs and asked a lot of new questions that I didn't know the answer to. "Where is Vincent now? Do you know when he left? Where is your daughter's car? Do you know anybody who might have a reason to do this to your daughter?" The detective asked me, "Do you know if your daughter was involved in drugs?" I said, "Babe hated drugs, cigarettes, and alcohol. She didn't want any of it in her house! And she didn't really like people who do use it, in her house!"

3:30 a.m., February, 8, 2002

Next the detective asked my ex and me to come down to the station and fill out a formal report. My present husband watched the kids for me, and we went down to police headquarters and answered the same questions. This time they put us in separate rooms while being video-taped at the same time. I left the girls in my apartment with Juan. When I got back home, I told my husband that there was nothing that he could do and that I couldn't sleep, so he could go back to work if he wanted to.

6 a.m., February, 8, 2002

I called my boss and briefly told her about my daughter (we watched each other's children grow up). I said that I wasn't sure when I was coming back to work. She said, "Don't worry about it, and just take care of your family."

Then I called my landlord, John, who had been contacted by the police a few hours earlier to get into the apartments. I said, "John, the police are here, and I found Babe in the closet of her apartment." John said, "Oh my god, Nancy, I'm so sorry!" I said, "John I can't sleep here another night. Do you have any other apartments available?" John said, "No, Nancy, I'm sorry, but I'll make a few phone calls and call you back later." John and his partner owned a few houses that they managed and repaired together. I had met both of them and their wives; they were the best landlords.

What was I going to do with my time now? There were so many things going through my head. I had no place to sleep tonight, and all of my friends that I would like to talk to were at work.

Then the phone rang, I said, "Hello."

"Hi, this is Rick, Vincent's, brother." (I was thinking what in the hell does he want, and why is he calling me? How did he get my telephone number, and besides, I had never met this person before in my life!) I said, "Yes?" Rick said, "How is Babe?" I was dumbfounded and fuming at the same time, I said, "What makes you think that there's something wrong with Babe?" Rick said, "Somebody told me that Babe was deceased."

I do not know how I was able to maintain my composure, but I said, "Yep!" Immediately he started crying and screaming in the background, "*No! No! No!*" I could hear him crying, yelling, and screaming, "*No, no, no!*" Then the line went dead.

That was very odd, but before I had time to react, the phone rang again. I said, "Hello" (this was a female voice), and she said, "Hi. This is Rick's wife, Sandy." (I could hear Rick in the background crying and vomiting very loudly.) She said, "Is Babe all right?" I said, "You already know Babe's dead, that's why Rick is vomiting and crying!" She said, "We don't know anything about her death." Then I said, "I didn't say that you did it, but you believe that it is true, or Rick would not be crying like that!"

Sandy said, "If there is anything, we can do please call us." (I have no idea who this person is, or what her motives are for calling me.) I do not know how much she knows, or how involved she may be. So, I said, "Thank you. Give me your number, and I'll give you a call if I need anything." She gave me the first three numbers then I heard another woman's voice, which sounded just like Vincent's mother saying, "Don't give her your number. She probably has caller ID anyway!" Then we were disconnected. So, I immediately called *69. The first three numbers were the same that Sandy had given me, and I got the last four numbers. Then I called the police. I told them about the two strange phone calls I had received.

6:30 a.m., February, 8, 2002

Next, the property owner called me back with good news. John said, "I don't have any apartments, but I do have two houses if you would like to look at them." So, I told him that we would meet him at the first house after I got the girls up and gave them some breakfast (two hours). The first house was in Avon Lake. The second house was much larger, but it was back in Elyria, only a few blocks from where we were trying to leave.

9:30 a.m.

On the way to the second house, Taliyah was talking to me. She talks very well for a three-year-old, and she talks a lot, but I was not really listening very closely. My mind was full of millions of other details that I was having a hard time processing. I was trying to sort out the different circumstances, suspicious phone calls, and the traumatic sight of my daughter's body stuffed into the closet that seemed to haunt me! It was as if I was trying to put a puzzle together in my head, but I had not seen all the pieces yet.

Suddenly Taliyah said, "Then he punched her in the face with a knife!" I said, "What did you say?" When she repeated it, I slammed on the breaks, pulled off to the side of the road, and really listened this time to what this three-year-old little girl had to say. She told me about an argument between her mother and her father that had changed from screaming to punching, and then the punching switched to her father having a knife and stabbing my daughter. My three-year-old granddaughter told me, "I tried to stop him from punching Mommy with the knife." She said, "I threw the cat at him to make him stop, and Big Boy scratched Daddy and then ran away!" My god! This poor little three-year-old girl watched her daddy stab her mother to death! I cannot even imagine what that might have been like. How can a normal adult live with that in your memory, let alone a three-year-old girl?

CHAPTER 3

Police Involvement

I decided that after we looked at the second house, we would go to the police station. I comforted Taliyah by telling her, "We need to tell the police everything we know so that they can help us find mommy!" (The girls did not yet know that I had found her in the closet. They did not know that their mother was dead.)

10:30 a.m., February, 8, 2002

When we arrived at the police station, I told the officer at the desk that we were looking for the girl's mommy, and that they had told me a story about a fight and a knife. Of course, they let us in. They had a special officer that talked to little kids. The officer took Taliyah into an interrogation room to take her statement, where they would then tape her as she talked.

As I waited in the waiting room with Amaya, we played a little bit, and then we looked at some magazines. But she couldn't talk yet, so the wait was very boring for her. Soon she started to fall asleep in my arms. We had only been there about fifteen to twenty minutes, but it seemed like an eternity.

Suddenly Amaya began to shake. I said, "Honey, what's the matter? Are you all right?" She was having a grand mal seizure. Her entire body jerked. All of her limbs were flung out for a split second each time. She had intermediate bouts of rigidness, slight foaming at the mouth, with loss of control in the bowels and bladder.

10:50 a.m.

I screamed for someone to call an ambulance. There was a fair amount of scurrying around. I yelled again, "Did someone call an ambulance?" Then the chief of police came in and told me that the ambulance was on the way! As Taliyah gave her deposition, Amaya stopped shaking; she took a deep breath and went completely limp. "Oh my God! Baby, please don't die!" I slapped her on the cheeks slightly and said, "Wake up, baby! Wake up!" I screamed, "Where is the fucking ambulance?" Once again, the chief of police scurried about to find out where the ambulance was.

Just then, he said, "The ambulance is here!" I ran out the back door with the baby and into the back of the ambulance. A few minutes later, someone came out with Taliyah. She climbed in with us, and we were off to the hospital. Taliyah looked at me and said, "Is my sister going to die?" I got a little teary-eyed, but I choked down my emotions once again. I did not want them to know that I was scared too. I wanted to seem confident so that they would be calm. I said, "No, baby, we are going to take her to the hospital, and they will make her all better." Amaya regained consciousness in the ambulance; she was very groggy and disoriented. I reassured her that everything was going to be all right.

11 a.m., February, 8, 2002

This was not quite ten hours after coming home from work. My life had been permanently changed in less than ten hours and would continue to change for the next fifteen to twenty years!

The EMS technicians drew blood, installed an IV, and took all the vital signs of Amaya, and even gave her a toy to play with. We were all at the hospital for hours. They took x-rays and ran numerous other tests.

Amaya was tired, weak, hooked up to an IV, electrodes, various monitors, and breathing through an oxygen mask. With her sister holding her hand, gently caressing her cheek and saying, "It's going to be okay, baby." I thought that I could not bear another moment of this tension.

My entire world had been crushed in front of me, and every time I turned around, another major tragedy awaited me. I wanted to cry so badly, even if just to relieve some stress, but those girls needed me to be strong. No matter how bad I felt or how tired I got, what those girls went through was far worse than the mountain of pain I felt.

I made a few phone calls. I let a few of my close friends know what was happening. I talked to my boss again to let her know that it may be a few weeks before I could come back to work. I talked to my ex-husband, and he said that he would be happy to take care of the girls for a few days. That was good since I had nowhere to go. I could not sleep in the new house yet, and I knew that I could not spend another night in my old apartment. My girl friend Karen asked me to stay at her house as long as I needed. She said that I could come and go as I pleased. She did not want me to be alone. Both she and her husband were always good to me. That was great because my husband was still out of town.

4 p.m., February, 8, 2002

When we got home from the hospital, I called and arranged for my ex-husband to pick up the girls. When he came, he told me that he would take care of the funeral. I said, "Thanks." I was not ready to deal with those details. I told him, "That's fair, if you pay for the funeral now, then I would pay for the girls for the next fifteen to twenty years."

There was a heart-wrenching message on my answering machine from my mom. She was crying and understandably confused. My mother was going through her own form of hell; my dad was in the late stages of Alzheimer's and did not really know who I was anymore. Dad still remembered Mom; they had been together for over fifty-two years. With her at his side, he did very well. I called her back and told her everything. She cried; it was all too much to deal with. I also asked her if she would call the rest of the family for me, to inform them. She said that of course she would.

After I hung up with mom, the police called to inform me that Vincent had just been picked up and was in custody. Of course, he denied everything. He said that he drove her to work on Wednesday (February, 6, 2002) and dropped her off in front of the factory she worked at, by the front door.

CHAPTER 4

Night Is Coming

By now, I was so numb emotionally that I refused to let myself cry. I did not want to think about finding my daughter. I was scared to start crying. I felt that if I started, I would not be able to stop. I was saving it all for the funeral, where I could let go and mourn.

6 p.m., February, 8, 2002

It was going to be dark soon; I had to get out of this apartment. You see I lived in a large house. My daughter Babe had the entire first floor, I had the second floor, and we both shared the basement. My living room was directly above her living room, where the entire fight took place. If I had come home right after work that night, I might have heard the fight. If I heard the fight, I definitely would have stuck my nose in their business. I could have knocked at the door or called the police or something. As darkness approached, a great wave of anxiety fell over me. I had to get out of there before it got dark.

I still hadn't had any sleep since Thursday (February, 7, 2002) morning at about 10 a.m. I had been awake for at least thirty-one hours so far, but I could not conceive of one single reason why I would want to close my eyes with the extreme probability of my daughter's body in the closet being the main attraction of my own private recurring nightmare. I called my girlfriend Karen and told her that I would be over soon.

When I arrived at Karen's I walked into Karen's house, her dog Max treated me as if I had known him just as long as Karen had. This was the first time in the three years that I have known Karen that her dog Max did not try to attack me. I think he knew something was wrong. Karen gave me a big hug, she was crying, her husband gave me a hug and her daughter too. Her daughter was Babe's age (but she had never met Babe).

We talked for a couple of hours, then watched TV for a few more. Karen and her husband had to go to work the next day so they went to bed at about 10 p.m. I couldn't sleep. Every time I tried to close my eyes; I could see Babe in the closet. Anytime I tried to get some sleep I would have a nightmare about what the fight must have been like, or what else he might have done to Babe. So, I just stayed up and watched TV all night.

8 a.m., Saturday, February, 9, 2002

In the morning, when Karen's family got up, they thought that I had gotten up early, but I had never slept. We gathered around the table for breakfast, and then in came the first newspapers. They spelled my daughter's name wrong. Her name was Babe, and the paper spelled it Bebe. This gave me something to think about besides the obvious. Jim and Karen read the newspapers. I merely looked at the headlines. I had my toast and tea, while they informed me of the crap in the paper before going to work.

Karen's sisters came over to help her paint the kitchen floor, so I went back to my old apartment to make a few phone calls. I tried to organize stuff and start packing. I knew that I was never going to spend another night in that apartment again.

12 noon, February, 9, 2002

It was very difficult to concentrate on anything; my mind kept coming back to Babe. I didn't eat much, and the police evidence van was still in my daughter's apartment. I was just doing busy work. I was trying to keep my mind off my ongoing problems. I tried to get my head together, but that seemed too great a task for me. I must have wandered around my apartment for hours aimlessly without actually doing anything. I went into the basement to get the remainder of the laundry that I had started on Thursday morning. I found that the clothes that were in the dryer were now gone. I checked out the washer to see if I had left anything in there, and I found a small paring knife. I took it upstairs to the police and told them where I found it. They told me that they had found some sheets with a lot of blood on them in the dryer and that they had sent them to the lab for testing. I told them that the sheets were mine, and the blood was from a large menstrual accident.

3:30 p.m.

David (my ex) called me and asked me for half of the money for the funeral. I said, "What? I don't have any money." I told him that after everything settled down, I would see what I could do.

4 p.m.

I went back to Karen's house well before dark. After dinner, we sat in the living room and watched TV. I tried to keep my mind off things. I started to feel a little paranoid. Am I acting normal? Has anybody noticed that I have not slept? I was screaming for help on the inside but in complete denial on the outside. I felt as if I had been on a three-day bender, and I was lost with no ride home. Where were all my drinking buddies? When did the party stop? Why wasn't I having any fun?

10 p.m.

I needed some sleep. I was ok while my friends were awake, watching TV, and talking to me. But I was afraid to go to sleep. Every time I closed my eyes, I could see my daughter's dead body stuffed in the closet. Now at ten o'clock on Saturday night, I had not had any sleep since I woke up Thursday (February, 7, 2002) at about ten o'clock in the morning. I had been awake for sixty hours straight, with not so much as a nap. Every time I closed my eyes, all I could see was the body of my daughter stuffed into the closet. It was as if it was painted on the inside of my eyelids. The most horrible thing that I had ever seen in my entire life, and I hope I never see anything like it again, was now permanently etched on the inside of my retinas.

I was so very cranky and paranoid that I began to drink some Bacardi to relax. I drank until I absolutely could not stay awake! I wanted to be in a self-induced coma, so I couldn't dream, or if I did, I wouldn't remember it in the morning. Finally, at about two o'clock in the morning, I couldn't stay awake anymore! I needed some sleep; I had to go to church in the morning. I increased the alcohol content of my drink and chugged it. I had finally made it impossible to stay awake; after sixty-four (64) hours, I finally fell asleep.

8 a.m., Sunday, February, 10, 2002

In the morning, I got up, had some tea, and got dressed for church. I felt a lot better (even though I only had about six hours of sleep); some were better than none. I was supposed to move today. The lives of two entire households had to be packed, moved, and unpacked in less than ten hours. I was not sure how I was going to accomplish that but it had to be done.

12 p.m.

Immediately following the church service, some of my church family asked me if they could do anything to help us. I answered, "If you have a few hours to spare, I could use a few extra hands to help me move!" Shortly after I got home to my old apartment, I realized that maybe half of my church had shown up to help us move. The minister's wife helped me by organizing everything in Babe's apartment (so I never had to go back in there). I had asked her if she could please save anything (which was useable) that I might need to take care of the girls. My mother, her aunt Elaine, and Elaine's daughter Melissa organized the new house. I asked them to put stuff anywhere that they wanted, as though it were their house. I could always move something later if I did not like where it was. My daughter Jane was helping, and some of my close friends and even my ex-husband pitched in. That left *me* to try to organize my old apartment.

There were literally so many people helping between my apartment, Babe's apartment, and the new house, that I only had enough time to stand in one spot, in my apartment, and give directions to those doing the moving. I could tell them to keep this, throw that away, or what room items go into, in the new house. It was as though I was standing in the center of a hurricane (the only calm spot), and my entire life was swirling around me at an incredible speed. The girls did not have very many clothes. Almost all their clothes were taken by the police (blood evidence); they took *everything* with blood on it.

6 p.m.

We quit for the day just before dark. As we were about to leave, we saw spectators driving by the house slowly. I don't know what their morbid curiosity hoped to see. We needed to lock up 'cause after unloading the last load, it will be dark. This time I went back to the new house instead of Karen's house.

This place needed a lot of cleaning. The previous tenants were smokers and had lived here for twelve years. My husband and I scrubbed down the walls to get off that twelve years' worth of smoke and tobacco residue. I thought that the new house would keep me busy and take my mind off things. During the days, I would make curtains for the windows and unpack boxes. At night, I would cook, feed the girls, give them a bath, and try to get them to bed so that I could watch some TV.

Monday, February, 11, 2002

The days would go by faster now, with lots of new and/or extra jobs to do. All of the family members were coming in at different times. My mother came in from Montana on Saturday; my daughter Jane came in from Youngstown on Sunday. My daughter Cyndi came in from Florida on Monday. My son Wayne was coming in unexpectedly from Germany (he was in the Air Force), on Monday afternoon.

My ex-husband called me and wanted to arrange a meeting tonight, to tell Taliyah about her mother. Taliyah still thinks that we are looking for her mother. She saw the fight and probably lots of blood, but her mother was still alive when she went to bed. She did not know that her father, Vincent, finished her mother off sometime on Wednesday morning (February, 6, 2002); he slashed her throat as she lay in bed. The mattress was saturated with Babe's blood; the carpet was too; in fact, the blood had gone all the way through the mattress, box springs, carpet, and floorboards to the basement floor.

There were only a few drops on the basement floor or I would have seen it on Thursday when I had done laundry, which is why the clothes were all over the Babe's bedroom floor and all over her bed to cover up the blood.

Amaya was too young to understand all of this; she could not even talk yet. I wanted to break it to them gently, but they had been staying with my ex-husband since Babe's death. So I didn't have a chance to talk to them. However, my ex-husband insisted that Taliyah *must be told!* I was *very opposed* to this. If I didn't agree he would do it anyway, without me. So, I agreed, reluctantly.

He also asked me again for money for the funeral. I told him, "My lawyer said that I don't have to give you any money!" He was so ticked off that he could not contain himself. He threatened to take the girls away from me. I laughed at him, told him that he was an idiot, and hung up!

That night we all gathered at my ex-husband's house. There was my ex-husband David, his wife, their minister, my mother, my son Wayne, my daughter Jane and her two kids, my daughter Cyndi and her baby, Babe's two girls, and me. After everyone was settled in, I sat and watched. I said nothing at first. I listened as David's clergywoman tried to talk to Taliyah calmly and rationally as you would an adult. She may have used smaller words, but much the same manner as you might with an older child or an adult.

Taliyah was fidgety and did not want to listen. She started out with, "Honey, your mother is not coming home, she's gone."

"Where?" asked Taliyah.

"She is in heaven," they told her.

"*No!*" she said. They told her, "She's gone."

"*No! No! No, she's not!*" Taliyah yelled to them. When they tried to make her pay attention, she got agitated. So finally, my ex-husband blurted out, "Your mommy is dead!" Everyone looked shocked, and Taliyah said, "*No, she's not!*" So again, my ex said, "Yes, honey, your mommy is dead." Now Taliyah yelled, "*No, she's not!*"

I could not stand it any longer; they were torturing this poor little three-year-old girl with a subject that she was not ready to deal with yet. I spoke up as she was fighting, screaming, and trying to get away. And I said, "I found your mommy today."

Now I had her full attention, she looked at me very calm now and said, "What?" Very calmly and quietly, I said, "I found your mommy today."

"Come here, and I'll tell you about it." She sat on my lap. Everyone was very quiet as I explained, "We have looked for your mom for a few days now and could not find her. So, I prayed to Jesus to please find her for me." Taliyah asked me, "Where did you find her?" I said, "Jesus went to her school and took her up to heaven!"

This was all she needed to know for the moment. She was much calmer now. For the time being, she did not need to know more. There was no need to explain to her about her father. There was no need to explain to her how her father killed her mother, or how he stuffed her body into the closet. A three-year-old child does not need to understand fully all the secrets of life. A three-year-old child should not easily understand the same truths, which most of us adults, cannot or do not want to understand. She knew enough to deal with the funeral. Everybody was satisfied that she knew enough, so we all went home.

When we got home, my mom had gotten a call from my brothers (Rick and Tim); they were taking care of my dad so my mother could come to help me. My mom and dad lived in Montana, and my father had Alzheimer's. My mom took care of my dad by herself, with a small amount of input from my brother Tim. Tim lived next door to them. When mom was at my house, Tim had his hands full, so my brother Rick (from Atlantic City) went to Montana to help him.

While my mother was away, my dad freaked out, "Where is Evelyn?" "When is she coming back?" "Why is she gone?" etc. My mother tried to calm him down over the phone, but his understanding nature was gone now. It has been replaced by paranoia.

My father was in a terrible place in his life also. So I got on the phone with him and tried to appeal to his long-term memory. I said, "Daddy," talking like his little girl. "This is Nancy!" He said, "Where's your mother?" I answered, "Daddy, I need Mommy here for a little while." My father had a lucid moment and said to me, "I'm sorry for all your troubles." Then just as fast he said, "I need your mother here!" My mother was heart-broken. It choked me up to hear my father like that.

Mom was torn between a husband who needed her so desperately and the funeral of one of her grandchildren who died excessively young. My mother felt that her place was with me in this time of need, but my father was paranoid and becoming violent. Therefore, she had to leave the next day, the day before the funeral. My daughter Cyndi said, "We don't have any nice clothes to bury Babe in." So I gave her my credit card and told her to buy anything that she thought would be appropriate. Afterward, Cyndi took the dress to the funeral home.

CHAPTER 5

The Funeral

Tuesday, February, 12, 2002

The day before, at the showing… Mom went home on Tuesday, and just before the showing at the funeral home, my brother Victor came into town. I picked him up at the airport; my god, my brother Vic looked so much like Dad that I almost did not see him by the baggage claim. We went to the funeral home for the showing. Everyone I knew was there. This was a closed-casket ceremony of course. My daughters asked me if I wanted to look at Babe before she was buried. I had spoken to one of the detectives who were at the scene and asked him, "If this was your daughter, would you want to see her?" He answered me, "No, ma'am, I would not!" I told my daughters, "That was good enough for me. I had seen too much already." I wanted to remember her as she was. However, I told them that if they felt that they needed to see her for themselves, that that was their decision. My oldest daughter Jane was the only one who went in to view Babe privately and say goodbye.

All of Babe's friends were there. All of the major executives, from the factory we worked at, were there. In addition, there were coworkers from her shift, as well as some from my shift were there. My ex-husband, his family, friends, and all three of his ex-wives were there; along with me, my husband, my other three kids, Babe's girls, my brother Victor, and all of my close friends. I mingled the entire time that I was there. There were so many people there that if I had not walked all around the funeral home, I would not have seen everyone. Most people, who knew Babe, knew me, through her. I could not just sit by the coffin with my ex-husband all night.

Vincent's mother and father came. I don't know why, but I did not expect to see them there. His mother gave me a hug and asked me if they were allowed to come to the funeral. I said, "Sure, I don't think that you wanted this to happen!"

After we got home, my brother and I talked late into the night. I put the girls to bed, and later my brother Victor went to bed. This was the night before the funeral and I still needed to write the eulogy. This was something that I told my minister I needed to do. So that night, when everybody else was in bed, I wrote it.

This eulogy came easily to me once I started writing it. I kind of knew what I wanted to say before I started. I wanted to say goodbye to Babe, and I wanted to try to express the feelings of others that attended but were maybe unable to speak out publicly themselves.

Wednesday, February, 13, 2002

The actual funeral… In the morning we all visited. I had not seen my brother Victor in at least three years. We were up late the night before talking, and then I wrote the eulogy, so I was tired. After breakfast, we have to take baths, get dressed, and a whole production. It has been a long time since *my* kids were small. Even the simple things like getting in the car to go somewhere took thirty minutes.

On the way to the funeral, my husband said, "Would you like me to have Vincent killed?" I said, "What?" My husband explained that he did not know anyone who did that type of thing, but he knew people who did know those sorts of people. I thanked him for the offer, but I told him, that that was something that I could not be a part of.

We all arrive at the funeral home. (The press was outside; they wanted to film inside, and my ex-husband said no; there were maybe 100 to 150 people more than I expected.) Inside we all exchanged pleasantries and were seated. As the ceremony began, everybody started to cry. I could hear my ex-husband crying and my children crying, and I could hear my best friend Janet wailing uncontrollably in the background.

Many (understandably) fell apart. This was finally supposed to be my chance to grieve (the opportunity for me to allow myself the luxury of completely falling apart). The air was thick with emotion, and just as I was about to lose my composure, I looked down at those two adorable little girls, with panic in their eyes, as they saw everyone they counted on falling apart. When their eyes met mine, I took another deep breath, smiled at them, and gave their little hands a small squeeze, and once more, I choked down my own tears.

They did not need one more person in their life who could not look them in the eyes without pity. Then the minister, Steve Carmany, asked me to come up. Quietly Steve said to me, "Nancy, you don't have to do this." I looked at him and said, "Yes, I do." I got up in front of a few hundred people. As I began to deliver the eulogy, I was a little choked up. When I first got up there, I felt that first big wave of fear, and I felt the temperature in the room skyrocket, and my eyes welled up. I took a deep breath and stopped looking at the crowd in the eye. This was not the time to cry yet!

The eulogy went like this:

The Babe I knew

As a mother, Babe was strict, loving, and dutiful. She worked the system for every dollar and advantage she could get for her two girls.

As a wife, Babe was always supportive, patient, and faithful, and she really meant, "Until death do us part!"

As a sister, Babe was always loaning her siblings' money, which she knew they would never pay back, to make sure Mommy had a nice Christmas present.

As an employee, Babe was prompt, abided by the rules, adhered to company policies; she always made rates! She volunteered to help at the company Christmas parties, for hours, and hours, and hours!

As a coworker, Babe was funny and always had spare time to harass and tease her fellow workers.

As a cousin, Babe was always available and supportive.

As a friend, Babe loved to talk on the phone for hours.

As a student, Babe was diligent and persevering.

As a daughter, Babe visited on holidays. She called to help, called to complain, called to borrow money, called to get a babysitter, called to borrow stuff, and sometimes she called just because she was bored.

The Babe I knew called me *freak*! It was my privilege to witness her as a mother, sister, coworker, daughter, and friend. I watched her grow up from that shy, quiet, curly-haired little girl in glasses, into a mature intelligent woman with the confidence it takes to set her goals and achieve them! And I am *very proud.*

Whenever Babe called me, or I called her, she would always answer the phone, "Hello, freak!" But every time she was ready to hang up, she would always say, "I love you, Mommy!"

After the funeral, we all went to the cemetery. We, of course, had a front-row seat. After all the people were filed in, our minister, Steve, began to speak. Taliyah said, "What are we doing here?" And I said, "This is your mommy's funeral." She said, "What's in the box?" I said, "Mommy's in the box!" She asked me, "What are they going to do with the box?" How do you explain to a three-year-old the concept of putting your loved one in a box and burying that box six feet in the ground? I panicked for a second. I looked up at the sky and thought, *God, please put the right words in my mouth.*

I looked into the eyes of Taliyah, and I said, "When we are all done here, and everybody has said their goodbyes, then they will put the box in the ground. Then later just like a seed, when the rain comes, and the sun shines, God will take Mommy up to heaven, and He will make flowers grow where we put the box."

Taliyah said, "Do I call you Mommy now?" I said, "No, honey! You call me Grandma." Then she asked me, "Well then who's going to be my new mommy?" I told her, "Nobody, honey. You only get one mommy. Nobody can ever take the place of your mommy." She came back with, "Then who's going to take care of us?" I said, "I will take care of you, and you two will stay with me forever." Then she asked, "What about after you're dead?" I told her, "Honey, I am not going to die until you and your sister are both fat old grandmas." I am not sure they believed me at first, but that was not going to be the only time I said those words.

Next was the funeral dinner at my church. Most of the family, friends, and church family were there. Once again, my ex-husband, this time accompanied by his wife, approached me. "Well," he said, "when can I expect some money?" I said, "At Babe's funeral? You're going to ask me for money at my daughter's funeral?"

Previously I had discussed this issue with my husband Juan; he told me that if David asks you for the money again, I should tell him that we would pay for the entire funeral. All he has to do is give us *all* the receipts, and we will pay 100 percent.

Therefore, I said, "My husband told me to tell you that we will pay for the entire funeral." My ex said, "You don't have that kind of money!" I said, "What do you care where we get the money from?" "Give us all the receipts, and we will pay everything!" I never saw the receipts and never paid a dime. That was the last time I offered to pay for the funeral, but that was not the last time that the cheap bastard would bring it up!

C H A P T E R   6

Nightmares

Friday, February, 15, 2002

Soon after the funeral, I noticed the girls were starting to have nightmares. Amaya would have more than one a night. She would wake up screaming, but she couldn't talk yet, so she couldn't tell me about her dreams. Taliyah would always tell me the same thing, "The black monster was chasing me, trying to kill me." Both girls were having bad dreams *every single night!* They would wake up screaming every night. Sometimes they'd wake up many times in one night. They weren't getting a good night's sleep, and neither was I!

Sunday, February, 17, 2002

After a few days of this, I had to find a good counselor for the girls. I could see that there were deep psychological wounds involved. At the time, I had no idea how deep. A day or two later I saw a friend of mine, Pat. He is a guidance counselor in the public school system. I had told him about my recent circumstances. Pat said that he had read about the story in the paper but that he had not known that it was about me. I told him that I knew he was not the kind of counselor I needed, but I asked if he could recommend someone to me. And if possible, I need it free. Pat took my phone number and said that he would let me know.

Monday, February, 18, 2002

The next day, Pat called me back; he had arranged for me to meet with the counselor. Bellefaire JCB, this was a charitable organization. It was all set up that the girls could come as often as the counselor deemed necessary and stay in therapy for as many years as they might need, free of charge. This was a real godsend to me! I filled out all the appropriate paperwork for them to start sessions. At first, we went twice a week. I answered a lot of questions and watched as they did play therapy. Later I had to stay in the waiting room, while the girls had their sessions.

With all of this going on, and very little sleep of my own, the stress started to take a toll on me. I began to vomit every day. It was hard to eat. When I *was* hungry, I ate, but later I would be nauseous. I wouldn't let the girls see me cry, and I was never out of their sight. I had no time to grieve on my own. I'm sure that is the reason for my vomiting every day. I started having coughing jags, where I could not stop coughing until I vomited. I realized that with a sip of water, I could stop the coughing jag. But I had lost thirty pounds before June. I was more concerned for the girls' welfare than mine. After they were stabilized, I would worry about my problems, but in the meantime, I might finally lose the weight that I have always wanted to lose.

My days were full of appointments with Child Welfare, Social Security, and the food stamp administration. None of these agencies could be satisfied with one visit. Each of them required more and more info. I would have to go somewhere else to get that info and go back to the first three places at a later date. I also had to see a lawyer for custody; luckily, I have a good friend, Kurt Sarringhaus, who is a probate attorney, so I could set up guardianship of my two granddaughters.

Thursday, February, 21, 2002

I am starting to get phone calls from the police detectives and the district attorney office. The detectives want to either ask questions or give me information. The district attorney wants to do the same. At night I am becoming obsessed with Court TV, specifically the *Forensic Files*. I would watch it, thinking that I might learn something that I might need to know for the eventual trial.

So many times, I would have a nightmare that would wake me up, and not be able to go back to sleep. My husband, Juan, was not able to deal with my emotional stress. If I felt a crying jag coming on, or wanted to talk about my bad dreams, he got very distant. I needed some way to vent all my pain. If I was unable to go back to sleep, I would turn on Court TV, a movie, or a situation comedy, until I was ready to go back to sleep.

Friday, February, 22, 2002

One night I had a dream about Babe… I was in the bathroom looking in the mirror. I was talking to my husband who was sitting on the toilet, and I heard something. I opened the door and looked down the hallway. I could hear someone coming up the stairs. It was Babe, and she had Taliyah on her hip. She came down the hallway and into the bathroom with us. She walked right up to me, face to face, not more than three inches away. I said, "Aren't you going to say something?" Babe said, "I don't have anything to say!" Then she handed me Taliyah and walked away. I never had another dream about Babe again.

Saturday, February, 23, 2002

In the morning, I called my oldest daughter Jane to tell her about my dream. I asked her if she ever had dreams about Babe. She said that she was having nightmares. In her dreams, she saw Babe the way she was in the coffin. Cyndi was having dreams too, but because she did not view Babe in the coffin, her dreams were more like Babe never died, or like a shared memory of the two of them in high school.

Friday, March, 1, 2002

This was my first day back at work. I had been off work for three weeks now. I am more than a little scared. I am a bartender, and usually, I can talk to anyone, but lately, *I do not want to talk to anybody*. Taliyah and Amaya will go back to school on Monday. We had all been out of the system for three weeks. I couldn't believe that it had only been three weeks; it felt like it had been months since my life was normal.

The first couple of days back at work were easier than I expected. Naturally all my coworkers knew what I had been through, but my customers didn't. If they asked where I had been, I just told them that I had a death in the family and left it like that. But I was surprised at the number of people who wanted more details. They would say something like, "Oh, I'm so sorry, and who died?" I would say, "My daughter," and hope to leave it like that. But they would say, "Oh my god! How did she die?"

I could not believe that my customers were being so invasive. I knew them too well to be rude to them but not well enough to pry into my private life. If they were really good friends of mine, they would already know. If I could have told them that she died in her sleep, or some other lies, and discreetly say that I'd rather not talk about it, it would have been a lot easier. But I couldn't get those words out of my mouth. It was impossible for me to lie about it. I was still in too much pain, and far too angry, to sugarcoat the truth. So, my answer was, "She was murdered!" Of course, there was a barrage of questions as a result of that statement. They always wanted to know, "How did it happen? Do you know who did it? Have they caught him yet?" etc.

This would set me off on a story of events that took almost an hour to tell. And this story had been told many times since. Nevertheless, *every time* it took the same amount of time to tell. I always tried not to tell it, but I noticed right away that once pushed into telling the story, I could not stop until I had gotten all the way to the end.

I believe that this was my form of therapy. With all my new commitments, and taking care of the girls, I had no time to grieve or go to therapy.

My old duties
Go to work.
Take care of the house.
Try to get a new business off the ground.

New duties
Feed, dress, and bath two small girls
Lots of extra groceries
Doctor's appointments
Immunizations
School teacher meetings
Visits to therapist, bi-weekly
Kids having daily nightmares (getting no sleep)

Weekly visits to the district attorney

In addition, numerous phone calls to various agencies either calling me or me calling them, trying to get as much information as I could.

I was so busy that I did not have any time for myself. It was difficult to talk to any of my friends about all of this because the girls were always around me. I felt like I couldn't do this at home, so my bartending job became my therapy. I didn't need advice yet. I just needed to talk this out, get it all out of my system. I needed to get rid of all of my anger with Vincent and my frustration with the system and relieve the stress of all my new commitments.

Therefore, I talked about it to anybody who asked me about it. I did not instigate any of these conversations, but if they asked me, I was physically unable to keep my story silent. I was so compelled to tell them the entire story of how I found her body stuffed in the closet and could not stop until I got to the part where they caught her husband.

Once, I noticed that my boss could hear me telling the story again, but I was powerless to stop in the middle of the story. I had to tell them all my feelings about the crap I got from Medicare, the hoops I had to jump through with SSI, food stamp administration, etc. I had to produce proof that my daughter was dead and prove that I was the girls' permanent guardian. I still, occasionally, had to prove that I am their guardian, showing my copy of Babe's death certificate, the girls' birth certificates, yada, yada, yada.

The girls seemed to be okay at school. They had both told people about their dad. If we were shopping for groceries, and someone calls me their mom, they will say, "That's not my mom! My mom is dead! My dad killed my mom!" This would, of course, shock anyone who made the mistake of asking that question. The girls had a right to express their feelings, but it was quite horrifying to watch. I could see the pain and anger in their eyes and hear it in their voices.

Sometimes I would say to the girls, "These people don't know about your mom. They don't know that I am not your mom." And I would say, "You don't have to tell everyone about your mom if you don't want to." I understand that they have many unresolved anger issues, and I tried to channel their energy into something less disturbing, but this was their reality.

CHAPTER 7

Government Involvement

Friday, March 15, 2002

My minister's wife told me that I might be able to file for some money through the Victims of Crime program. This might help me out a lot. Although the girls' nightmares had slowed down, there might be a lifetime of repercussions to think about. Amaya still has nightmares a few times a week, and Taliyah has about one a week, but that was still better than several per night, *every night!* The Victims of Crime lawyer was very nice, but just like any other government benefit, there were a lot of hoops to jump through, forms to fill out, many more trips to the lawyer, and a lot of time to wait.

Tuesday, March 25, 2002

Just as I was getting used to the new pace of things, and I thought my life had quieted down some, I got a letter in the mail. It was addressed to me, but it was from someone I didn't know. As I opened the letter, some photos and a business card fell out. I don't know these people, and the business card was from a lawyer that I had never heard of. The letter began, "Dear Ms. Seberiano, please let me offer you my condolences for the death of your daughter Babe." She went on to say that she had talked to Babe about a year before, and that she had been with Vincent years ago and the photos were of his first two children. She told me that Babe was eager to get the oldest two children together with the youngest two children. In addition, she had hoped that I might find it in my heart to arrange a meeting someday (I don't think so).

She went on to say how she (like my daughter) wanted something better for her children, so after she left Vincent, she went on to law school and became a lawyer up in Cleveland. She offered me her legal services. She had each of her two children write a short letter to me. Maybe I'm letting my imagination get the better of me, but I'm having a hard time trusting strangers, especially ones from Vincent's past.

In her letter, she mentioned that she is still in contact with Vincent's parents. I saved the letters, photos, and the business card too. You never know when that information may come in handy. However, at this time I had no intention of meeting with or speaking to this woman or her kids.

Monday, April 1, 2002

My eldest daughter Jane decided to move in with us for a while, to help. Her husband and kids came too. Jane helped a lot around the house. One night we were getting supper ready, and someone spilled some cherry Kool-Aid on the floor. Taliyah just stared and stared at it. My daughter told her to go to the other room. However, she was frozen, unable to move. I believe that she had some sort of flashback. I picked her up, carried her into the other room, and asked Jane to clean it up quickly. When I came back, I said that maybe it looked a lot like blood to her and tried to prevent that from happening again. Now I was more able to get a little sleep with Jane in the house. I think that Jane was able to sleep a little better too!

Thursday, April 11, 2002

Today was the probate court hearing. My lawyer, Kurt, called this one a slam dunk. He said that this was merely a formality and that I should have no problems at all. I said, "Then why do I have to be here? Why couldn't we just turn in the paperwork to be legal?" He told me that I did not need to go in but that I needed to be present just in case someone else showed up to claim the kids. I said, "Like whom? Nobody knows that I am here." Kurt told me that he was legally obligated to inform Vincent of the guardianship of his children and that he may have asked his parents to be here.

Nobody else came to claim these little girls. Nobody else ever expressed any interest in taking over full responsibility and care for these two desperate little girls. No one was willing to make the kind of sacrifices that it would take to make a difference in the lives of these two little girls. They had no one else in the world that cared about them except me. That was good for me because I did not have to deal with a custody battle, but a very sad thing to look back on for the girls. No one else was willing to make any sacrifices for their welfare. It was very hard for me to realize that what came so easily for me to do without a second thought was too great a sacrifice for anyone else to think about doing. Make no mistake about it; I am *no* saint. It was just the right thing to do, as though I had no choice in the matter at all.

Tuesday, April 30, 2002

After a few visits to my friend Kurt (the probate attorney), all the guardianship papers were done. However, right down the hall, about three doors was another friend of mine Paul Matus. I had not seen Paul for a few years. In an ironic coincidence of fate, Paul is also the county coroner. I went to his office because he performed the autopsy on my daughter. His secretary told me that he was not in. She said that I could leave a message, but I told her that I would come back another day.

I was also notified by mail that the jury trial was set for July 30, 2002 at 8:30 a.m.

Thursday, May 9, 2002

My mom called to tell me that one of my favorite uncles had died, Uncle Tippy. Of course, we all went to the funeral. I was able to see a lot of my relatives who couldn't make it to Babe's funeral. They were surprised that I came. I wanted to pay my respects to a man I loved very much. I wanted to get out of my house, with all of my problems. My parents and siblings were all out of state and were unable to attend.

I felt that I must represent my family, and as I sat back watching the service, I noticed that the girls had a reverent demeanor; they seemed to grasp the importance of the occasion already at their young age. They asked me who died, and I told them that my Uncle Tippy died. They asked me who that was, and I told them that they had never met my uncle. "But you know his wife!" I said. I pointed Aunt Pearl out to them, and Taliyah said, "She must be very sad." It made me choke up to hear her and how much of the world she truly understands already at less than four years old.

We sat in the back, and the girls fell asleep waiting for the end of the service. Then as everyone paid their last respects before leaving, I asked one of my cousins to watch the girls so I could go up and pay my respects. I went up, stood beside the coffin, and looked at my Uncle Tippy for the last time. I reached in and touched his hand, as I did at all the funerals, of all my other loved ones (just not Babe). I stood there and stared at him for what seemed to be a long time (I think that it was only a few seconds). He looked so peaceful like he was sleeping.

I wish that I could have seen my daughter, all made up this way, sleeping peacefully, with that pink light they put on you so you look alive. However, with all of my daughter's cuts and bruising, that was impossible to make her look like she was only sleeping. I did not have the chance to touch her hand, tell her face to face how much I loved her, or say goodbye to her and grieve in the way that only a mother can.

Sunday, May 12, 2002

Before you know it, it was Mother's Day. I felt very strongly that the girls, and I had to go to the cemetery to see Babe. We bought a large wreath to put on her grave. This was the first time that we had been back to the cemetery since Babe died. The grave was still somewhat fresh looking, and the dirt was lumpy with not much grass growing on it yet. You could see a few small holes from the ground settling.

We put the flowers on her grave; there was no tombstone yet. The girls asked me, "What do we do now?" I said, "You could talk to Mommy". Taliyah got down on the ground to look inside one of the holes. I said, "What are you looking for?" She said, "Mommy!" I said, "You can't see her in there." She's in heaven now. "Then what are we doing here?" she asked. I decided to show them how *I do it*. I face the tombstone reverently. I address the deceased by name, I may describe my life since the last time I had talked to this person, but I think these girls are just too young. I talked to Babe for a minute or two, and just as I began to get very teary-eyed, the girls said, "Can we go now?" and we were off.

C H A P T E R   8

Attempting a Distraction

Sunday, May 26, 2002

The oldest girl, Taliyah, turns four years old today. I tried to make it as happy as I could. We had a small private party, with Chinese food, cake, and ice cream. My daughter Jane was there with her two kids, my two girls, and Jane's cousin Richie; we all had fun. We talked, we danced, and we reminisced about Babe and all the good times we had together.

Friday, May 31, 2002

Memorial day, we got up early today because we are going to take a trip to Hershey, Pennsylvania. We are going to see the chocolate factory, and all the kids are very excited. We drove for hours and stopped just before we got there to get a hotel for the night. In the morning, we will see the factory and then go home.

All the kids were so excited about spending the night in a hotel with a pool. After checking in, we all went to the pool and swam for a few hours. Then we went back to the room and called for pizza delivery. When we started getting ready for bed, everyone had to take turns in the shower. When all were done and clean, Amaya went to the bathroom last to tinkle. We waited, and waited, and then I went to see what she was messing with in the bathroom. However, the door was locked. I said open the door. And I heard a small voice inside say, "I can't Gamma." Now, sterner, I again told her to open the door. Again, I hear a small and now slightly whimpering voice say, "I can't open the door, Gamma!"

Being a hotel, it does not have the kind of lock that can be easily picked, as I did when my children were small. Nor does the doorjamb allow the use of a credit card to open the door. After exhausting all my options, I called the front desk. The girl at the front desk was very courteous and said that she had a special key that would work. I went to the front desk to pick up the key, but there was no place on the door to put it. There was no keyhole or special place in or around the doorjamb to insert the specialized key. Therefore, I called the front desk again. This time the very courteous girl at the front desk was more than a little condescending, perhaps her youth and inexperience may have been the problem, but she said to me, "Ma'am, you just put the tool into the hole in the doorknob." I informed her that there was no hole in the doorknob! She replied, "There has to be!" I said, "Come down here and look at it. There is no damn hole in the freaking doorknob!"

In the meantime, I tried to instruct Amaya on how to unlock the door. However, she was far too young to understand my instructions, and she lacked the hand-eye coordination necessary to unlock the door. She was trying, she was crying, and she was scared. She kept saying, "Gamma, get me out! I want to go out! I'm so tired, *Gammaaa*!" I tried to comfort her through the fireproof, burglarproof door, but I was scared too. I could see her tiny fingers under the door reaching for me. I could touch her, but that was all I could do.

The girl from the front desk could not believe her own eyes that there was no way to open the locked door. I told her to call the fire department. She said, "I don't think that I am allowed to do that." I said, "You call whomever you have to, to get this approved, because my little girl in there has a seizure disorder, and if something happens to her, I will own both you and this hotel!" She called me back from the front desk and told me that the fire department was on its way.

This was supposed to be a time of relaxation for me and the girls. Just as I was about to start to cry myself, while holding on to that tiny hand under the door, "I said the firemen are coming. Let's try again one more time. Just pull on the little button, and open the door." Then I heard the door unlatch. "Yeah! The door is open!" I called the front desk to tell her that everything was okay now.

The rest of the trip was extremely fun, educational, and very high caloric but otherwise uneventful. It was somewhat hot on Memorial Day weekend and a little crowded, but it was also a much-needed change of pace. We purchased a lot of candy and souvenirs, and we all learned a lot about chocolate. I looked forward to the long drive home; I was not in a hurry to get back to reality.

CHAPTER 9

Insurance Company

Wednesday, June 5, 2002

The insurance company did not make any contact with my lawyer or me at all. One of us should have heard from them by now. My lawyer, Kurt, sent them a letter asking them if they need more information or something. After four months, they should have sent us some sort of correspondence.

Monday, June 10, 2002

The insurance company called me today and asked me questions as to the suspicious circumstances of Babe's death. I answered, "There were no suspicious circumstances. She was murdered, and *I* found her body in the closet." I asked, "Do you think that she stabbed herself to death and then stuffed her own body in the closet after?" The insurance investigator told me sternly, "Ma'am, we have the right to investigate all claims, especially during the first two years. We can take as much time as we need to get all the proper evidence." He also stated, "Besides, your file was just thrown on my desk *today* (June, 10,

2002)!" After four months, this insurance company is only now assigning the case to someone.

He was asking me for information, which had already been mailed out by my lawyer months ago. I informed the man that all of *that* information was sent out months ago. I also told him that one of the girls has a seizure disorder, and if something happens to her because of lack of this money, I would go to the press and inform them of the obvious negligence of his company.

The following morning, I called my attorney and informed him of my recent telephone conversation with the insurance company.

Friday, June 14, 2002

I got a letter from Vincent's court-appointed attorney, addressed to Taliyah. It says, "I have been advised that you are a witness to Vincent White's case. Please send to my office a statement of what happened and what you can testify to at his trial." I called the assistant district attorney on the case, Tony Cillo, and he told me that I did not have to tell the other person anything.

Friday, June 21, 2002

Kurt sent the insurance company a follow-up letter stating that the murder was on February, 6, 2002. In addition, a list of items:

- ❖ A claim forms
- ❖ Newspaper clippings
- ❖ Police report
- ❖ Death certificate
- ❖ Autopsy report
- ❖ A copy of the three previous letters of request

❖ Moreover, a note detailing the phone conversation (of May 30th) with a representative of the company asking if they need further information

❖ Finally, a phone call to a company representative who informed us that the insurance company was contesting the claim

My lawyer informed them that he was leaving on vacation for two weeks, and that if the funds and the appropriate interest due were not on his desk when he returned, he would be initiating legal proceedings against the company, to obtain the proceeds, the interest, and an appropriate amount for punitive damages for bad faith dealings.

Friday, June 28, 2002

All four of my grandchildren were playing outside on the back porch when all of the sudden, Taliyah ran in and said, "Amaya has the shakes!" I said, "What?" I ran outside, and the little one was having another seizure. I asked my daughter Jane to call an ambulance. I picked up Amaya, took her into the kitchen, put her on the kitchen table, stripped her down, and cleaned her up while I waited for the ambulance. I informed the ambulance driver that she had been diagnosed with a seizure disorder (febrile seizures), and he told me that it was unnecessary to call an ambulance for this reason. He suggested that I just make her comfortable, make sure that her air passage is clear, and just wait it out. He said that is all I can do. Her doctor said the same thing on another episode. They all told me that this is something that she will outgrow. How do you just sit back and watch a grand mal seizure, watch the child take a deep breath at the end of it, and then it looks like she is dead. This is not normal! Moreover, I will never get used to it!

The next day I searched the Internet for a specialist at Rainbow Babies & Children's Hospital that would see my girl. I went to Amaya's pediatrician; she said, "I don't know what you expect me to do." I said, I would like a referral. I would like to know for sure if this is something that she is definitely going to outgrow. On the other hand, is there something else that we need to do? Therefore, I made an appointment with the Chief of Pediatric Neurology at Rainbow Babies & Children's Hospital in Cleveland.

Sunday, July 7, 2002

I got a call from Vincent's mother. She asked me, "Can you see it in your heart to let us see the girls?"

She has some nerve, who in the hell does she think she is? Perhaps her children did not talk to her about everything, but Babe told me lots. For example, on January 6, 2002 (one month before Babe was murdered by Vincent), I received a call around midnight, from Babe. She said, "Mom, can you come and pick me up?" I asked her where she was. She said that she was in Oberlin at Vincent's mother's house. I got directions from her and my husband, and I went to pick her up.

After the kids and Babe got into the car, Babe said that she went there to drop off Christmas gifts for Vincent's family. Babe was only planning to be there for an hour or so. Vincent borrowed the car to pick up his brother (a ten-minute trip) and never came back.

Vincent's mom did not turn up the heat for Babe or the babies. She would not feed them or let Babe use the phone. She said that the phone was out of order; she received calls, but calls will not go out. She would not give Babe a ride home or anywhere else. Babe did not have very many diapers, extra formula, or extra clothes. Vincent's mother successfully kept my daughter and her children at her house for nine or ten hours. They were all cold tired and hungry. I took them home, fed them, and helped her put the kids to bed. Even if Vincent's mother hated Babe, she should take care of her own grandchildren. In addition, if she did not want my daughter in her house, she could have let her call me earlier. After all that she had put my daughter and her two babies through, on just this one occasion (what about other occasions?), how can she have the nerve to call me and ask for any favors at all!

Now after remembering all of that, I politely asked her, "Where did you get my phone number?" She told me that a girl at Value City Furniture, who knew Babe, gave it to her after we were recently in the store. With that tidbit of information in my pocket, I told her, "After the way you treated my daughter, you and your family will never see these girls again!" His mother said, "We loved Babe. We were always so good to her!" I said, "Please!" and I hung up!

The moment that I hung up with her, I called Value City Furniture. I asked for the manager, and the person answering the phone said, "Ma'am, there is more than one manager here. What can I do for you?" so I said, "I have a problem that I can sue your store for, now who do I need to talk to?" After a few moments, a man came to the phone. I told him that one of his employees had given *my* phone number to the family of the man that stabbed my daughter to death.

I remember that girl's face because she made a point of telling me that she knew Babe and that she was so very sorry for what had happened. The Value City manager asked me, "What do you want me to do?" I said, "Fire her!" I said, "If I had given away personal information about any of my clients at my job, do you think that I would still have a job?"

I was so upset by the last thirty minutes' worth of phone calls that I called my good friend Karen. I said, "Do you have any booze?" She said, "Yes," and I asked her if she would come over, and I unloaded on her. I was so pissed off! I should have sued Value City Furniture! I could have sued them for thousands of dollars. We drank for an hour or two, then I thanked Karen, and she left. I just needed to vent.

Monday, July 8, 2002

The life insurance company waited until the day that my lawyer was to come back from his vacation before they drafted their next letter saying that they were so sorry for the delays on the case.

Tuesday, July 9, 2002

Appointment with the pediatric neurologist at Rainbow Babies & Children's Hospital. Dr. Bass is the best in her field. She informed me that the febrile seizures that Amaya was having were something that she would outgrow. However, I asked her, "How can you be so sure without some sort of test?" She assured me that she has seen *so many* of these cases that she can be sure. I asked her to run whatever tests she need to do to eliminate the possibility of something else being wrong. Her dad was on crack; I do not know if he had done something to Amaya, or if he had smoked that stuff around her. There could be other causes, and I just wanted to eliminate all of them.

We scheduled a sleep deprivation test. They hooked electrodes all over her scalp, then after she was asleep, they turned on a strobe light directly over her head in an attempt to cause a seizure. This test then reads the brain's impulses during the seizure. *If they can cause a seizure with this process*, then Amaya may have other problems; if not, then this is indeed something that she will outgrow. Amaya had no such reaction; we were all ecstatic.

Trial Preparation

Thursday, July 11, 2002

The girls and I went to see Tony Cillo, the assistant district attorney. I was able to unload a little with Tony about the trouble I was having with the insurance company, visiting the pediatric neurologist, and of course the phone call from Vincent's mother.

Tony wanted Taliyah to become a little familiar with the courtroom so that she would not be scared. He chitchatted about school and stuff with her. Tony told me that he was the same age as Vincent. He grew up in the same area and has known Vincent for quite a few years. On opposite sides of the law, Tony said that this was not the first time that he had had a run-in with Vincent. He said that he had never had enough to put him away.

Taliyah was noticeably nervous when asked to take the witness stand. There were only the girls, Tony, and I in the courtroom. What would happen if the court was in session, and this was the trial? I did not want her to testify at all, but Tony informed me that she was the only eyewitness. I asked, "Why can't she be in another room and give her testimony on a closed-circuit monitor?" Tony told me about the *defendant's right to face his accuser.* "That's not fair!" I said. "He has more rights than one of the victims." Taliyah did not want to talk into the microphone at all, not even for this practice run, in an empty courtroom.

Tony and I did not want to leave it to chance. Taliyah might not say anything at all on the witness stand, leaving the jury with reasonable doubt. I could not take the risk that the monster that had ruined so many lives could get off Scot-free. Therefore, we set up weekly visits to Tony's office. We went often enough for the girls to become friendly with Tony. He asked questions every time we went to see him so it was normal for him to ask many questions.

Thursday, July 18, 2002

I received a copy of Vincent's statement. I read his version of what happened. This dumb ass is a crappy liar. The phrase, shit for brains, comes to mind.

He writes, *I went home Tuesday, February, 5, 2002) (5:30 p.m.) after three days of partying, and my clothes were on the back porch.* Vincent states that his wife, Babe, told him that she was through and that since he was never home; he should move out. He said that Babe told him that she promised me that she would put him out for good. Vincent said that he asked her if there was someone else (*this is where he was trying to set up an alibi*); he said that she told him that she would not give him that information.

(My daughter worked forty hours a week and went to school twenty hours a week; she had no spare time or energy for an extra man, and it was slanderous to my daughter's reputation.)

5:45 p.m. on Tuesday

Vincent states that Babe let him into the house; he said that she was supposed to go to school at 6 p.m., but they ended up making up instead.

Well… that is not the way it happened. I was there on *Monday not Tuesday (February, 4, 2002) (3:30 p.m.)* Babe told me that she was sick and tired of Vincent's crap and that she wanted him to stay out permanently. I asked her, "What made this time different than any other?" She said that Vincent had been gone for three days without as much as a phone call.

I asked her what was stopping her from doing it, and she told me that he could just get back in the house any time he wanted to. "I can't lock him out!" she said. I asked her how does he get in, and she showed me a window in the basement that he could get into without breaking it and alarming the neighbors or me upstairs. I said, "Do you want me to fix this window so that he cannot get back in?" Babe said, "Yeah, if you can." I told her that her mom could fix that problem so easily. I went upstairs to my apartment, got a hammer and a few nails, and I nailed that window permanently shut. I told Babe that neither Vincent nor anybody else would ever get in that window again without some major help.

Babe thanked me and asked me if I would babysit the girls when she went to school; of course, I told her yes. She said that she had to feed the girls and get ready for school first, so I went up to my apartment.

5:30 p.m.

Vincent showed up; I could hear him talking downstairs. I went down to see if Babe needed any help. He was trying to convince her to give him another chance. After ten or fifteen minutes, they went inside to talk. I thought to myself, *Damn it. She let him back in.* I went upstairs for a few minutes, then at 5:45 p.m., I called her to see if she was still going to school or not. Babe was not the one to answer the phone; Vincent *always* answered the phone when he was there. I always had to ask if I could speak to Babe. Babe told me yes, she was going to school, and yes, she did need a babysitter. I thought that this meant that Vincent was not staying, or he would be watching his own kids. I told her to send the girls up. A few moments later they climbed up the stairs to Grandma's house.

5:55 p.m.

I called back to Babe's apartment. "Are you going to school or not?" She answered a quiet, "No," and I hung up. She took him back! If I had even suspected that he was capable of killing her, I would have done whatever it took to keep him away from Babe, even if it meant breaking the law. It is amazing what kind of heinous thoughts go through your mind after something like this.

10 p.m.

I called Babe again. I said, "I am bringing the girls down now." She said that she would meet me at the door. I carried the girls down one at a time and said goodnight. That was the last time that I physically saw my daughter alive. I was so disappointed in Babe. I did not want to *push* my way into her business, her marriage, or her life, but if she had only asked me for help, I would have moved heaven and earth. This might be stupid, but I was not afraid of Vincent. He knew that I had friends in high places. I think he was afraid of me.

Vincent's alibi goes on to say, *on Wednesday (February, 6, 2002) at 4:30 a.m., Vincent says that he asked his wife if he could take her to work, and she said yes. He claims that since the kids were asleep, both he and Babe agreed to leave them at home alone.*

The rest of this *did* happen on Wednesday after he killed my daughter. He left those babies alone in the house with their dead mother's body while he ran around.

In the rest of his statement, Vincent says that he drove Babe to work at 5:20 a.m. He says that Babe said she was going to make up the class she missed on Monday. Vincent states that on the way home, he got suspicious so he stopped at a payphone (around 5:50 a.m.) to call her work. He says that they told him that she never got to work.

Babe lived fifteen minutes away from work; he could have called from home. He was stating that thirty minutes later, he was on his way home to call. The factory that she worked at had a huge wall of glass where the entrance door was, and at that time of day, there should have been hundreds of people walking in the door with her.

Vincent states that he thinks Babe must be hiding at another man's house. At 6:05 a.m., Vincent found some drug dealer, rented out Babe's car to this drug dealer, and had the drug dealer drop him off in Oberlin. (Oberlin is thirty minutes away from Elyria, where his kids are.) Vincent says that he called his mother and father to pick him up, in town; they lived just outside Oberlin. His father picked him up. Vincent states that he was crying because he did not know where his wife was. Vincent states that he told his parents that he had to get back home because his kids were there. His uncles came over to pick him and his father up. He says that they went to a meat market (twenty minutes NW of his house), then to someone's house, then he states he asked his uncle to take him home. Vincent says that he arrived home at 11:30 a.m.

In his own statement, he left his children home alone (with their mother's dead body) for six hours.

Vincent then says that he fed his girls, cleaned them up, and cleaned the house, while he waited for his car to come back (Babe's car) at 2 p.m.

I was home on this Wednesday morning (February, 6, 2002), and the night before Babe had left a message on my answering machine asking me to call her when I got home. I called her at 1:30 a.m. (February, 6, 2002) and asked her what she wanted. Babe asked me to put Taliyah on the bus in the morning. That was the last time I ever *talked* to my daughter. I heard the bus come and go, and at about 9:30 a.m., I could hear the girls playing downstairs in their room. (The girl's bedroom was directly below mine.)

I got dressed and ready for work, and at 10:30 a.m., I left for Oberlin (work). When I got downstairs, to Babe's apartment, I saw her backdoor open and through the screen door, I could see Vincent. I knocked on the door to give him a message for Babe about a doctor's appointment for one of the girls. He said "Hi!" to me, and very uncharacteristically invited me in. I was very suspicious, I said, "No, thank you." He had never done that before. I wondered why he was doing it now. He said, "The girls are here," then said to the girls, "Grandma's here!" I declined entrance saying, "I have got to go to work," and I left. In hindsight, he may have wanted to get rid of me as well. He knew that I would be a problem. His statement said that he had a friend with him, but I did not see anyone.

Between the time that Vincent got home and the next time that he left, he states that he received three phone calls. His friend Jarvis came over (he says that he did not see me until almost 5 p.m.). He states that Babe's car was not back yet, and he needed a ride to go look for it. He says that his friend wanted a ride to his girlfriend's house in Lorain once Vincent gets his car back, and Vincent agreed. Vincent and Jarvis saw a friend a few houses down the street; they offered him gas money to drive them to the car. When Vincent got back home, he changed his clothes, then he, the girls, and Jarvis headed towards Lorain (7:30 pm).

When I got home on Wednesday night, sometime after dark (maybe 10 p.m.), I remember *not* seeing Babe's car in the driveway, and I assumed that Vincent had her car. I could hear the vacuum cleaner running and thought that Babe was staying up late cleaning because she was waiting for him to return with her car. She was usually asleep at about 9 p.m.

When they got to Lorain, Vincent states that Jarvis no longer wanted to go to his girlfriend's house. They ended up going across the street to a friend called Red. Vincent says that he cannot stop thinking about the whereabouts of his wife. They stayed there until 8:45 p.m., and then Vincent decided to rent out Babe's car again. He was dropped off at a friend's house down the street from his dad's house, where he, the girls, and his friend Jarvis stayed the night.

The next morning Thursday, February, 7, 2002), Vincent and Taliyah walked down the street to his parent's house (in Oberlin). Vincent asked his dad if they could all get a ride back to Elyria. He said no but offered a few dollars to ride the bus. Just then, his friend Jarvis pulled up with a girl going to Elyria. They got into the car, picked up Amaya, and went back to Elyria.

On the way home, Vincent remembered that he did not have his keys since he rented out the car, so he and the girls were dropped off at his cousin's house a few doors down from their house. Later Cousin Marcus came home, and Vincent cut his hair, his kid's hair, and another person's hair, and played some cards. They paid for the haircuts and sent Vincent to the store for cigarettes.

On Thursday morning (February, 7, 2002), I got up at about 9 a.m. I did quite a few loads of laundry. My apartment is on the second floor, and the washer and dryer are in the basement. I would come down my stairs and go down and around the back porch to an outside door leading to the basement (my entrance). When you go in the door, there is a set of steps immediately to your right, which go down to the basement. Straight ahead of you and up two stairs was Babe's kitchen door (*her* entrance to the basement). I listened at her door but heard nothing. Her car was gone, and nobody was home. I did laundry until time to go to work (11:45 a.m. I was running late).

On the way to the store, Vincent states that he stopped at yet another friend's house to have a beer. His friend took Vincent to get his car while the girls were not with him. As they were driving, they noticed that the police were following them. Vincent's friend pulled over, and the police informed them that they have to detain Vincent until they find out what had happened at his house. Vincent states that he did not have the slightest idea what was going on and neither did the police. Vincent states that the understanding was that someone called the police, saying that they could not find Vincent, his wife, his kids, or his mother-in-law. The caller felt that Vincent's wife and mother-in-law might have come to some harm at the hands of Vincent.

About 11 p.m., the dispatcher called and said to release Vincent; his mother-in-law had just come home, and she had the kids. Vincent states that while he was in custody the police searched his house. When released, Vincent went to his brother Rick's house. Everyone at Rick's house was crying and concerned about Vincent. He states that someone started the rumor that he had killed his wife and mother-in-law.

At 1:30 a.m. (February, 8, 2002), Vincent states that he walked to his friend Marty's house. He stayed the night and left at 7 a.m. When he left, he says he went to Burger King, the house of the girlfriend of his brother Stephen, and then to the bank to make a phone call. A few minutes later, this is when he says he was taken into custody for the murder of his wife, Babe.

(This is where I came home, and this whole story started.)

CHAPTER 11

Vincent's Mother

Thursday, July 25, 2002)

Every time I went to see Tony, we would have these vague discussions, kind of like a code so that the girls would not understand our entire conversation. Taliyah was very smart, and she would listen very carefully; she might not have understood everything that we talked about, but she knew that we were talking about her, her mom, or her dad. Tony would tell me any new information that he had. I would mention anything that I remembered, new problems that occurred, or discrepancies with the information that he told me.

I told him that I received Vincent's alibi from his attorney. I told Tony how full of holes his statements are. I informed him that I was physically there for some of the circumstances that he talked about in his statement. I saw the way some of these things actually happened, instead of Vincent's version.

Tony is the one who told me that, immediately after killing my daughter, Vincent called his mother. He told her what he had done, and she did nothing. She could have called the police in an attempt to save my daughter's life, and she did not! She could have anonymously called 911 to report trouble, and she did not! I asked, "Tony, doesn't this make her an accomplice?" Tony said we do not want his mother; we want Vincent. He was concerned about muddying up stuff and hurting the trial. Tony said, "She is just a sick old lady, and she could not have saved your daughter."

I told him, "She did not know that at the time, and she did not even try." I said, "What about those babies? You are not going to call somebody to do something?" I told him, "If my daughter called me and told me that she had just killed Vincent (even though I had never liked him!), I would have called the police, for her safety, his, and those little girls who might be in danger too. How often do these people kill their spouse, and then just finish off the rest of the family too!" I told him, "My point is that she did not know at the time that Vincent called her, if the girls were hurt also, or if anyone could be saved. She did not even try! Doesn't that make her an accomplice after the fact, or aiding and abetting in a felon?" Secretly I thought that I would sue her after the trial is over! I was angry enough to try to take everything she owned! I wanted justice and revenge, as well as their house and pension.

Tuesday, July 30, 2002

They postponed the trial until September, just before Labor Day. Now I have to wait even longer to sue Vincent's mother. I called Tony to ask him why was the trial postponed, and he told me that his lead witness (Vincent's mother) was having heart trouble. She just does not want to testify against her son. However, she is the one who told the police that her son called her immediately after the murder. Two days after Vincent killed my daughter, the police were looking for him; they showed up at his mother's house. That is when she told the police that her son called her right after he killed my daughter.

Vincent even tried to have his mother committed (for mental incapacity) so that she could not testify against him. After all that, the family has made it the responsibility of the district attorney to pay to have the mother's heart specialist on the premises during her testimony at the trial.

What a load of crap! I did not believe that she was that feeble. This is her second son in prison. Maybe this was guilt for not doing anything to help my daughter. Maybe if she were not such a witch she would not be feeling so feeble. Maybe remorse would be the thing to kill her finally.

Friday, August 2, 2003

My daughter Jane moved out. She and her family moved to another part of town. She, her husband, and her kids were a little cramped living here with us in our house. They need their own space. My husband and I helped them move out, and I gave her some of the furniture that I got from Babe's apt. They needed a lot of stuff.

Tuesday, August 6, 2002

I made an appointment to see Dr. Paul Matus (coroner) today. He gave me a copy of the autopsy report on Babe. I asked if I could see the photos taken at the time of the autopsy, and Paul told me that I could. He asked me if I was really sure I wanted to see them. Nevertheless, the trial was coming up, and there would be enlarged photos in the courtroom. In all the Court TV I had been watching, they always had photos blown up to two feet by three feet. I did not want to be surprised in the courtroom by enormous graphic photos. However, I decided to wait until I talked to Tony. I can find out what photos he will use in the courtroom, and then maybe I can look at them. Paul and I just got caught up a little and chitchatted about his family too. His oldest daughter is the same age as Babe.

Therefore, I told Paul that I was not ready to look at the autopsy photos yet. "Could I see them later?" I asked. He said, "Let me know when you are ready." I still have not seen them. I have not read the autopsy report yet either. These are details that I am not ready to deal with yet. How do you prepare yourself to look at autopsy photos of your daughter? How do you get ready to read an autopsy report, which graphically describes all the punches, lists and measures each stab wound, and explicitly details the manner, depth, and direction in which my daughter's throat was slit? I may never be ready! Somehow it is comforting to know that it will be waiting for me if I ever change my mind.

CHAPTER 12

The Actual Trial

8:30 a.m., Wednesday, August 27, 2002

This was the day set for the jury trial of Vincent White for the murder of Babe White. Taliyah was subpoenaed by the defense to appear for this trial on behalf of her dad. This lowlife scumbag wanted to use his own daughter, against her mother, to save his miserable ass.

On the first day of court, I was supposed to bring Taliyah to court with me, but I did not. After all, nobody was forcing me to. There was no police escort. There was no protection for a four-year-old against the press and their photographers or their idiotic questions. I understand the defendant's right to face their accuser, but the victim, especially a tiny little four-year-old girl who watched her mother being stabbed repeatedly, should never have to physically witness that person staring at her from only eight feet away, as she gives her testimony. Why does the scum of society have more rights than the victims?

Moreover, the press would have a field day with that kind of a witness. I was very careful to keep the children's names out of the press. I did not allow any photos of them either. The

D.A. told me there was nothing that I could do; she had to appear in court. So, I didn't bring her.

Maybe I could ask the judge to allow her to give her testimony via closed circuit TV in another room. On the other hand, the judge could clear all the press from the courtroom during her testimony, and she could be brought in and out through the back door. Nevertheless, I was at least going to *try* to prevent any more psychological damage to this poor little girl before I take her to court with me. Sometimes it felt like I was the only one in the whole world who gave a damn about her welfare, and the only one who tried to put *her* needs first.

I was there with one of my good friends Gay and my oldest daughter Jane Martinez; as we waited in the hallway, I asked the DA, Tony Cillo, "What are we waiting for?" He told me that they were waiting for Vincent to be brought in. Then they would try one more time to reason with Vincent and get him to confess so that we did not have to go through a trial. If he did not, then jury selection would begin. He said that the judge did not want to continue over the Labor Day weekend and sequester the jury. Tony said that holidays make the jury want to be done quickly instead of taking their time and doing a good job.

While the rest of us were waiting in the hallway, I noticed that there were others in the hallway that I did not want to see, like Vincent's mother. I saw her down the hall; the DA asked if I was all right. My heart was pounding out of my chest, but I told him that as long as she did not come up to me and say anything directly to me, I told him that I would be a good girl. However, if she did, I could not make any sort of promises.

Tony Cillo asked me why Babe married Vincent, after what he had done to her before. I asked, "Do you mean the fact that he punched her in the nose?" Tony told me that is not why he went to prison. He said that Vincent went to prison because he beat her up, broke Babe's nose, kicked her in the stomach a few times, ripped the phone out of the wall, and held her hostage for a few days.

My heart fell out! I did not know any of this before. I wasn't sure how to process this information. I was confused. Why didn't anybody tell me this before?

At that point, I was very happy that I had not brought Taliyah to court with me. We had all stood in the hall for well over an hour, perhaps two. The stress was exasperating, and the waiting was exhausting. I can't even imagine what it would have been like if I had to carry around a four-year-old girl as well. She would have wanted to visit with Vincent's parents. She would have had an endless number of questions.

Finally Tony came out with the news that Vincent took the plea bargain. I asked Tony, "What does that mean?" and he said that in a few minutes, we would all go into the courtroom, and the judge would read all the charges, Vincent would plead guilty, and it should all be over.

When we all got into the courtroom, my girlfriend, my daughter Jane, and I sat in the jury box (since there was no jury). Directly in front of us were the defendant and his attorney. To the left were the witness stand, the judge, and the bailiff. To our right were Vincent's family and friends, other spectators, and the press.

The court was called to session. Judge Glavas addressed the courtroom and asked everyone to be seated. The judge addressed the defendant and the charges were read as follows:

1. one count of felonious assault (minimum two years),
2. one count of aggravated murder (minimum five years),
3. one case of murder (fifteen to life)
4. one count of gross abuse of a corpse (minimum three years),
5. Tampering with evidence (fifteen to life).

That adds up to twenty-six years minimum. I was so happy because I thought that he would have no possibility of getting out for at *least* twenty-six years. By then the oldest girl would be thirty years old and probably married with a different name and be starting her own family. I even told my daughter (Jane) that was a relief that he would be in prison for at least twenty-six years.

Then I heard the judge say the words, "To be served concurrently." I did not know what that meant, but I was going to ask Tony as soon as I was able. Then the judge asked me as the mother of the victim if I would like to say something to the defendant before his sentence is handed down? I said yes, and I stood up and made this statement; "Your Honor, I believe that he should receive the maximum sentence possible for killing my daughter." As I choked back the tears I said, "He has destroyed the only person in this world who ever truly loved him and has caused deep psychological wounds to his daughters, and they may need counseling for the rest of their lives."

Tony Cillo (the DA) thought that it would be hard to give my impact statement. He told me not to talk directly to Vincent and to be careful not to get emotionally distraught or they would drag me out of court. I was glad Tony told me all those things. I kept thinking of them while I talked. The judge thanked me, and I sat down.

When the judge passed down the final sentence of fifteen to life, I was a little confused. I thought that there was a twenty-six-year minimum. After the judge left, we all remained seated and watched as Vincent was taken out in handcuffs, and I could hear his mother crying.

I asked Tony what the judge meant by *fifteen to life*; I thought when he read the charges that there was a minimum of twenty-six years. Tony said that *concurrently* means that he serves all of the terms at the same time. He told me not to worry that in these kinds of cases, the defendant is automatically refused parole for the first ten years after he is eligible. Tony said that he would serve a minimum of twenty-five years.

I could not help but feel cheated. Vincent should have gotten the death penalty. The lack of an actual murder trial was a huge disappointment, *very* anti-climactic! If there had been an actual trial and a full jury, they could have found Vincent guilty of premeditated murder, which is a death penalty offense. I was positive that he planned the whole thing. Why else would he have Babe call me and leave a message on my answering machine to call her back at such a late time? She would never have me wake her up (she would have just left the message without the need for a return call), but this way I would hear her voice; that was part of his *alibi*.

I believe that Vincent had made some sort of plan to get rid of her body, but maybe he could not get anyone to help him. Maybe then, he panicked. I do not know for sure what was going through his mind, but I know in my heart that he thought about this a lot. Maybe he thought about this very thing for two years, the first time he was in prison. He called her every day from prison.

I was happy that I did not have to put Taliyah through the trauma of the witness stand. I was relieved that I did not have to view those X-large photos of my daughter's body stuffed into that closet, the way that they always show on Court TV, or personally hear the coroner describe the assault and detailed information about the manner of suffering that my daughter had to endure. God forbid that her little girl should ever have to see those photos or hear those words.

However, I was already to let loose, cry, and bitch, get drunk and discuss the trial with my friends. This was to be my time to mourn. I had been looking forward to this time for seven months. This was the time to finally greave the loss of my daughter. I had arranged for someone to watch the girls all week. I had planned to be discussing the trial every day with friends at my house, crying uncontrollably, and getting drunk while I did it.

I did not want to be alone during this week and take the chance of my mourning getting out of hand. I wanted to be around people who knew me well and have only my best interests at heart. They all knew my plan. *Nevertheless, what now?*

I still had all this anger stored up inside me. I could feel an overwhelming wave of rage stirring up inside of me. I had planned to get out all my aggressions every night after the trial. The great relief that I had planned, to take this enormous burden off my aching heart, was crashing down around me. Once again, I felt that I had no choice but to choke it all back down inside.

The more I thought about it, the more it festered inside of me. After a few days, I was looking for revenge. I was looking for someone to take it out on. I was looking for someone to blame and hurt. Then it came to me. Moments after my daughter's death, Vincent's mother knew all about it and did nothing. That should make her an accomplice after the fact. I was going to try to sue her.

Thursday, September 12, 2002

I went to a good friend Tom Theado; he is a class action suit lawyer. I had known Tom for about ten to fifteen years at that time. At my appointment I gave him all the information he asked for. I wanted to hurt Vincent's family so bad. I wanted to take everything they had. I wanted to leave them homeless and destitute. I wanted to crush their spirit and force them into the same feeling of desperation that I had been feeling for so many months.

A few days later after investigating the situation, my friend Tom told me that he would not sue these people for me. He was not interested in pursuing this particular lawsuit. When I asked him why he told me, "They haven't got anything!" He said, "If I were to sue them and take everything that they have, that still is not enough to cover *his* expenses, let alone his commission, or my settlement." He said that quite simply their house is worth nothing; they don't own anything of value, and they have no savings or retirement.

Tuesday, September 17, 2002

My mom called and told me that Uncle Tom died (her sister's husband). They lived in Toledo, and we had visited them a few times over the years and saw them every year at the family reunion. However, with the amount of stress that I had been through recently, we did not attend this funeral, but that did not minimize the pain. My Uncle Tom will be missed.

Monday, October 7, 2002

My mother called me to tell me that my dad's cousin Marsha (who lives in a nursing home in Florida. with cerebral palsy and cannot attend to any of her own daily needs) was in a coma. I was beginning to dread my mother's phone calls. Lately it was nothing but bad news when she called. Anyways, my cousin Marsha had a DNR and was not supposed to be revived; we were supposed to let her go (her parents were already deceased). My parents were in Montana with my father's Alzheimer's progressing daily. The past is something that my father is still very familiar with, and he was quite distressed to hear about his cousin.

The hospital wanted to put in a feeding tube. My cousin refused so they waited until she was too weak to fight, and after a few days with no food, of course, she lost consciousness. That is when they put the feeding tube in any way. This was a lot for my entire family to go through. I had expected to be attending another funeral. With my mom and dad unable to attend, I felt that I could not miss this one. Marsha, her sister, my brothers, and I grew up together (even though she was older than I was by eleven years). After a few weeks, she got better, but it was a very long two weeks.

Friday, October 25, 2002

This was Amaya's birthday, and I had invited all of my close friends and her mother's dearest friends. All those who wanted to help me in any way that they could were babysitting so that I could work again. They were of course at the top of my list.

Because it was around Halloween, this was to be a costume party, so as we got ready for the guests to arrive, I put makeup on the girls. Taliyah wanted to be a witch, and the now three-year-old Amaya wanted to be a werewolf. I finished Taliyah's makeup, and she went outside to the backyard to wait for the guests to arrive.

For Amaya's makeup, I drew black lines on her face for the deep wrinkles and darkened her eyes, eyebrows, nose and hairline with black then added brown to blend in between her real face color and the dark black lines. Not a bad job if I do say so myself. All I needed was the fake rubber ears I bought at the costume shop and the medium brown hair spray to spray over everything to make the entire thing look very realistic for nighttime. When I was done, I held Amaya up to the mirror to see herself, and… she screamed, "*Monster, monster!*" I laughed, "What's the matter? That's you, baby."

"*No, no, monster!*" I could not get her to look at herself in the mirror. That was so cute and funny that she was afraid of her own reflection. Everyone came, and we had such a wonderful party. We had a small bonfire. It was truly a memorable time for everyone.

CHAPTER 13

Another Flood of Pain

Tuesday, November 5, 2002

My mom called me to tell me that my father had fallen and hit his head. His Alzheimer's had gotten to a crucial point one day when he told my mom that he thought that it was time to go. Mom was not sure what he meant, but he looked perfectly lucid. She told him that he could go if he thought that he needed to go now and that she would come later to meet up with him. Dad said, "I just thought that it would be nice if they came and found both of us lying here together dead."

This scared my mother very much; she had no idea what my dad was thinking. My mother told my dad that she had too much to do; she couldn't leave yet. "Nancy is having a lot of problems with Babe dying and the girls," and Tim (my brother) was having troubles with his wife being sick. She told my father, "This is just a really bad time for me to leave." My father said, "I just thought it would be nice if we went together." Mom told him that that would be wonderful, but there was so much for her to finish up before she could go. She looked at him lovingly, caressed him, and grazed her hand a crossed his cheek as she said, "If you feel that you have to go now, you don't have to wait for me. You can go now, I will be there very soon, and we will be together again."

My father really wanted them to go together, so my mother asked how would we do it guns and knives are so messy, and we have worked so hard to have a nice home. With the poisons around the house, if you don't do it right it could be quite painful and still not die. So, my mom said, "Let's go to the hospital and ask the doctors there. They will be able to help us with something painless and very quick."

My mother said that the front passenger door was frozen shut and told my dad that he should sit in the back passenger side. When Mom shut the door, she activated the child safety lock so that he could not open the door. She also latched his seatbelt for him; he was no longer able to figure out how to open it. Mom thought that this way he could not do anything to her as she drove.

When they arrived at the hospital, my mother said that it would all be over soon, and quietly, she told one of the hospital personnel what had transpired at home. The doctors gave Dad a sedative and informed my mother that he could never go back home again. It was far too dangerous for her and him.

He was taken to a nursing home in town, so Mom had gotten an apartment close by so that she could be near Dad. This is where he fell. He was just walking, and he misstepped. My mother told me that she had been informed by the staff that patients rarely regain consciousness from these types of injuries. Mom said that he might be gone soon.

Wednesday, November 6, 2002

With the impending birth of my fifth grandchild (so far, I had been in the delivery room with three of the first four), I had already booked my flight to Florida on the tenth. I told my daughter Cyndi that she had better hurry up and have that baby. I told her that I could only afford to come once; if she did not have the baby while I was there then I would have to miss it. I told her about her grandfather falling, the circumstances that that might bring about, and to keep him in her thoughts.

Thursday, November 7, 2002

Cyndi called me to tell me that her doctor was going to give her a C-section on Friday morning; she was more than a little scared. I tried to calm her down, and then I said that I would be there right after she got out of the hospital.

Friday, November 8, 2002

I got a phone call today, telling me about a bouncing baby boy. I was so happy for them; everything went fine with her delivery. I told her congratulations and said that I would see her on Sunday morning.

Sunday, November 10, 2002

I arrived early in the morning at Tampa-St. Petersburg airport. Amaya and Taliyah stayed at a friend's house for a few days. When I got to Cyndi's house, she had just gotten home from the hospital the night before. Cyndi looked good, and the baby was so tiny. I told her and her husband that I was there to help them catch up on their sleep. I told Cyndi that I could take the night feedings so that they could get some sleep. I remember how tired you can get when the baby wakes up every two hours.

Cyndi was recuperating from surgery too. They both thought they should be able to do it all on their own, and many people have, but you can only lose so many days of sleep in a row before it affects every part of your life. So, by the second night, I said, "Look, you guys. I'm only here for three days. I can catch up on my sleep on the way home. When I leave, you will have to do it all by yourself. I cannot come back later, so get your sleep now." The baby was so beautiful, and that was a nice visit.

Thursday, November 14, 2002

My mother called me at work; with the two-hour time difference from Ohio to Montana, it was sometimes hard for Mom to catch me at home. I was at the bar (my job) when she called. She said, "Your father passed away about four fifteen. He was very calm and died very peacefully." She told me that he would be cremated on Saturday. I said, "Can you wait for me? I want to see him first, to say goodbye." Then very humbly, I added, "Mom, I just got back from Florida with Cyndi's baby. I don't have the money to come." (That is a very hard place to be, when you have to borrow money from your mother to go to your father's funeral.)

8 a.m., Saturday, November 16, 2002

Both my brother Tim and my mother met me at the Montana airport. We went to breakfast and caught up a little. Then we went to the coroners. When we walked into the room, it was dimly lit. I was not prepared for my father to look like that. He was lying on a slab with a sheet over him. I guess I expected him to be a little made up, like at a funeral home. Dad wanted no frills, and no funeral, just cremation. That is what Mom and Dad both wanted. However, it is a very hard thing to look at. My mother was on my left, touching my father's forehead, and then she gave him a kiss goodbye. My brother Tim was on my right.

I tried so hard to look at my father and say goodbye, but it was very disconcerting to see another dead body. My father was completely unprepared, not at all the lifelike version you get at a funeral. They usually look like they are sleeping, or maybe like a statue from Madame Tussaud's Wax Museum. Instead, my father had that same dark mauve color that my daughter had. All the blood was congealed in his skin, and as I gazed at him, my daughter's dead body kept coming into my mind. I couldn't get it out of my head, as long as I looked at my father. I turned to my brother, grabbed his arm, buried my head in his arm, and said, "All I can see is Babe!" I cried for a second, but then my mother said, "Are you ready to go?"

I went back to my mother's apartment in town. We had dinner at some place in town, and there was an art festival in the local neighborhood by my mother's apartment. We walked around from exhibit to exhibit. When we got back to Mom's apartment, we settled in for the night; my plane was to leave in the morning.

Saturday, November 16, 2002

About 7 p.m. that night (Montana time), the phone rang. Mom said, "It's for you."

"It's for me?" I asked, "Who would call me here?" My friend Karen from Ohio called. (The one I stayed with when Babe first died.) I asked her what in the hell was she calling me for and why was she calling me here? She said that she was at her sister's house and that her dad died that day. I said that I was so sorry and that I wished that I could be there for her, in her time of need. She was really there for me, and I felt more than a little guilty that I was not there for her. I jokingly said that her dad could have waited until I got home. She said that it was okay, her mom and sisters were there, and she would be all right.

Sunday, November 17, 2002

The next day, I got home in the early afternoon. There was a message on my answering machine. "Nancy," sobbing. "This is Janet. Mom died. The funeral is Sunday night at 7 p.m." Oh my god, three funerals in two days. I quickly got the girls dressed; they knew Janet's mother too. Janet babysat the girls once a month so that I could go back to work. And frequently she would stop by her mother's house with the girls.

Five funerals in nine months? How can that be? That is so far above the national average. I have broad shoulders and can carry a tremendous load before I break, but how many funerals will these girls have to go through in their short lives? They have already been to too many.

I have physically been to four funerals and got heart-wrenching news about one that occurred while I was in Montana and the terrible ordeal with my cousin in Florida and her feeding tube. I don't know about you, but I don't know how much more I can put up with. If I ever see another dead body, it will be too soon.

CHAPTER 14

After the Holidays

Saturday, January 1, 2003

Somehow we made it through the holidays without a major catastrophe. Thanksgiving, Christmas and New Year's were all a great comfort and times of renewal. Times well spent with family and friends. After the year that I had just had, I am not sure how I lived through it, but I was so very happy that it was all behind me now and very much looking forward to the future.

Sunday, January 5, 2003

My husband who worked out of town came home twice a week. He came home Saturday night after work and stayed until Monday morning, and he would come home on Wednesday nights in the middle of the week. Today after church, we had lunch, watched a movie or two, and had dinner, and as I was washing the dinner dishes, Taliyah came to me and said, "Grandma, Grandpa touched my butt!" I said, "What?" She repeated, "Grandpa touched my butt!" I said, "I'm sure it was nothing, honey," in a dismissive manner.

If any other person in the entire world had said that to me, I would not have believed them, but I knew that this little girl loved him and was quite confused by his actions. I was sure that some way that he held her might have seemed wrong to a little girl, or maybe the way squirming little kids slide out of your hands when they want down can cause them to wind up being held oddly. I wasn't entirely sure, but I was certain that he did nothing wrong on purpose. Nevertheless, after what these girls had been through, I wasn't going to take any chances. I watched him very carefully after that. They were never left alone with him again, and when he was there, I kept a close eye on their interactions together. I noticed right away that he paid more attention to Taliyah than Amaya. And I say that when she would sit by him, he would make sure he knew where I was. I did not want to read more into this than there was, nor did I want to talk myself into seeing something that wasn't there, so I watched.

I was molested a few times as a child. That inappropriate touch, or the disgusting look that you would get from someone who was having unclean thoughts about you, to your face. I have never been raped, but I had been grabbed with the wrong intention, by people who were old enough to know better, many times.

I began to dread his coming home. One night when he came home, in the middle of the week, after work about eleven thirty midnight. We were all in bed. The girls were asleep, and I pretended to be as well. My husband was downstairs for a while, and when he came upstairs, he looked in on me, and then he went in to see the girls. He looked like he was just checking to see if they were all right. However, he stood there for quite a while. These were not his kids, he had never had any kids, and I don't believe that he had ever wanted any kids. Nevertheless, I did want him to try to be a real grandpa to them, and I thought that he was really trying. But he stared just a little too long and looked towards me. Was he trying to make sure that I was not awake? If you are not doing anything wrong, why do you care who's looking?

Thursday, January 9, 2003

I started to ask the tough questions. I asked Taliyah what Grandpa did. Without prying too much, I asked her, "When did he touch you?" She told me that when she would go to bed at night, she would go in to say good night to him, and he would open the covers to invite her in, she would climb in, and he would spoon with her (my words not hers). I knew that the way the legal system is if I ask the wrong question, Taliyah says, "Grandma told me!" and my husband gets off Scot-free.

I was immediately disgusted; it was too late. I thought that I was being careful, but I was already too late. I felt so bad that I had not protected her, but at least there had not been any penetration. The next Sunday at church, when it came time for prayer at the end of the church, I went up to my minister Steve Carmany. I started crying right away and said, "I have to get rid of another husband!" Steve asked me what happened. I gave him a brief explanation. He set up an appointment to talk to me the next day, then he prayed for me.

Monday, January 13, 2003

The next day I had a long talk with my pastor Steve. I told him everything. I cried and cried! I told him that I didn't know what to do. I loved him but I couldn't live with him. I didn't want to go through another divorce. Steve informed me that he broke the marriage contract, and I was not obligated to put up with that. He also said that I needed to put him out for the safety of the children. I knew that he was right, but I told him that I was not sure if I could do that. Steve told me that he had a legal obligation to report this. That eased my conscience a lot. I told Steve, "You do what you have to do."

So before the shit could hit the fan, I asked my husband to move out. No explanations. Just move out. He said then he wants a divorce. I said, of course, I would give you a divorce. But the night that I had made the decision to put him out was one of the scariest nights of my life. I had never been afraid of my husband before, but after everything that I had been through with my daughter Babe, and Victims of Crime telling me that the most dangerous time was when you asked them to leave. I was afraid to go to sleep that night. My husband was still in the house.

Steve called the authorities. They said that I needed to get a gynecological exam for Taliyah. Seriously, on a four-year-old girl? I called the doctor and made an appointment. I discretely took the doctor off to the side, so as not to make this too traumatic for my girl. The doctor said, "You realize I have to report this to the police." I told her that the police told me to come to have the examination done, but please feel free to do whatever she needed to do.

Next, we were talking to child services. They do not let you stay in the room with your child to comfort them while they talk to them. Taliyah did not want to talk about this. She had no problem talking to anyone about what her daddy had done to her mommy. However, this happened to her, and at her age, she understood that she did not want to tell everyone about this. It was so heart-wrenching to sit in the hallway powerless as they questioned her.

They told me that her statement was inconclusive. I asked, "How that was possible? Could I talk to her?" They said that she would have to give them the details on her own or they can't use them. I was not allowed to question her. All I wanted to do was be in the room during the questioning to make her feel safe and tell her that it was okay to tell them everything. But that was strictly forbidden. They informed me that Taliyah was too young to tell them how many times he touched her and approximately when this started so that they would know how long this had been going on.

After all, of this, then we had to talk to the police. Taliyah asked me why she had to talk about it again. "You said that if I told those other people (child services), I wouldn't have to talk about it again!" I reassured her that she needed to talk about it so that he could never do it to anybody else again.

The police called him in to talk without telling him what they wanted. I was not present at the time, but later the police told me that he passed the lie detector test. (How does that happen?) I suggested that maybe it was because he didn't think that he had done anything wrong. In addition, I don't believe that he completely understood all the questions they asked him. (One time he had been involved in a minor fender bender. I accompanied him to court, and I insisted on an interpreter. Later he told me that it was difficult to understand the inter-preter. I asked him why. Wasn't she speaking Spanish? He said, "Yes, but it wasn't Mexican. It's not the same.") Needless to say, that was the beginning of my divorce.

Saturday, January 25, 2003

The girls and I went to the cemetery today; it was Babe's birthday on Thursday, 23rd. She would have been twenty-six years old. We went to the cemetery for the funeral. We went for Mother's Day and took flowers. We all got out of the car, and I noticed that the tombstone was there now. It was a very nice stone, but something was very wrong! Babe's middle name had been misspelled. Her father ordered the monument for her grave. How can this be true? I can understand the press spelling her name wrong all those months ago, but how could her father? *Is it still wrong today? Yes,* it is!

Saturday, February, 6, 2003

I received a frantic call from my ex-husband, "Amaya has had another seizure!" I told him that I would be right there. I drove to the hospital. He and his wife were quite shaken up. This was the first time that they had ever seen her have a seizure. I told them that she was all right. I informed my ex that she had had quite a few of these, and I had taken her to the best pediatric neurological surgeon at Rainbow Babies and Children's Hospital in Cleveland. After much insistence, along with numerous tests and evaluations, I believe them when they say that this is something that she will outgrow. They have all convinced me that this is not that serious; still it was very hard to watch and not be concerned.

(Living in the Present)

Nowadays things are a lot better. Both of the girls have stopped having nightmares about Vincent. Taliyah is now twenty-five years old. She was on the honor roll, sang solos and duets with her sister in the church, and still tries to take care of her little sister. She still remembers some of that night but not everything. Amaya is now twenty-three years old, was on the honor roll, sang solos and duets in the church with her sister, and is in love with life. She cannot remember anything about that night. The sad part is that she does not have any good *or* bad memories; she has no first-hand memories of her mother at all. They don't even remember the funeral.

As for me, I cry all the time now. I cry every time we go to the cemetery. We go on Mother's Day and Babe's birthday (January 23rd). The girls feel so secure now, and I weep a lot around them. When the girls sang in church, my face was red… my eyes were puffy… and my shirt was wet! I am so frequently choked up when I hear them sing that I cannot sing myself. I can't help but think how proud I am and how very proud Babe would be to see what beautiful human beings they have grown up to be. I cry at movies and even some commercials. I even cry when I look back at recent photos and wish that Babe was here to share those memories with us.

I have a collage of photos of Babe in my living room. There are pictures of her with Cyndi, Wayne, and Jane at every age. There are pictures of her with her babies, Jane's babies, and even her when she was a baby. She is the common denominator in every picture. These are the photos that I was supposed to take to court with me. The DA told me that I needed to make the jury feel like they knew her. He asked me to bring one or two photos, but I found that I could not limit myself like that. There were three pages of photos.

I even cried a lot when I wrote this book. I had to uncover a lot of old scars, but I cry the most when I think about the girls' futures. There are going to be a lot of recitals, plays, school functions, parties, and events that Babe will miss, and I will cry at each and every one of them. But most of all, when I think about them dating, going to the prom, going off to college, or getting married, I am already crying. Even now, my face is red… my eyes are puffy… and my shirt is wet!

Nancy Seberiano is a mother of three daughters and a son, and a grandmother of nine grandchildren. Nancy was a forty-five-year-old bartender at the time of her daughter Babe's death. She has since moved to the Amish countryside and spent the last twenty years in a more peaceful atmosphere. She volunteered at the local food pantry and newspaper, was a caregiver for her mother before her passing, and even did a stint on the village council. Nancy loves to cook, sew, and paint in her spare time.

Nancy has always been a believer, and her faith in God has been her only saving grace through many difficult times in her life.